PERICLES

Other titles in the
RULERS OF THE ANCIENT WORLD series:

ALEXANDER THE GREAT
Conqueror of
the Ancient World
0-7660-2560-8

CLEOPATRA
Queen of Ancient Egypt
0-7660-2559-4

HANNIBAL
Great General
of the Ancient World
0-7660-2564-0

JULIUS CAESAR
Ruler of
the Roman World
0-7660-2563-2

RAMESSES II
Ruler of Ancient Egypt
0-7660-2562-4

PERICLES

Great Leader of Ancient Athens

Don Nardo

Enslow Publishers, Inc.
40 Industrial Road
Box 398
Berkeley Heights, NJ 07922
USA

http://www.enslow.com

Library of Congress Cataloging-in-Publication Data

Nardo, Don, 1947-
    Pericles : great leader of ancient Athens / Don Nardo.
        p. cm. — (Rulers of the ancient world)
    Includes bibliographical references and index.
    ISBN 0-7660-2561-6
    1. Pericles, 499–429 B.C.—Juvenile literature. 2. Statesmen—Greece—Athens—Biography—
Juvenile literature. 3. Orators—Greece—Athens—Biography—Juvenile literature.
    4. Greece—History—Athenian supremacy, 479-431 B.C.—Juvenile literature. 5. Athens
(Greece)—Politics and government—Juvenile literature. I. Title. II. Series.
    DF228.P4N35   2006
    938'.505—dc22

                                                                    2006001743

Printed in the United States of America

10 9 8 7 6 5 4 3 2 1

To Our Readers:
We have done our best to make sure that all Internet Addresses in this book were active and
appropriate when we went to press. However, the author and publisher have no control over and
assume no liability for the material available on those Internet sites or on other Web sites they may
link to. Any comments or suggestions can be sent by e-mail to comments@enslow.com or to the
address on the back cover.

Illustration Credits: ©Ancient Art & Architecture Collection Ltd/Topham/The Image Works,
p. 100; ©Ann Ronan Picture Library/HIP/The Image Works, pp. 25, 75 (top); ©ARPL/HIP/The
Image Works, pp. 3, 27; ©The British Museum/Topham-HIP/The Image Works, p. 93; Clipart.com,
pp. 58, 94, 103; ©Corel Corporation, pp. 75 (bottom), 136; Enslow Publishers, Inc., pp. 6, 118; J. G.
Heck, ed., *Heck's Pictorial Archive of Military Science, Geography, and History,* published by Dover
Publications, Inc., in 1994, design at the top of pp. 7, 13, 29, 45, 62, 80, 97, 115, 131; ©Mary Evans
Picture Library/The Image Works, pp. 15, 43, 53; Shutterstock.com, pp. 72, 138; Time Life
Pictures/Getty Images, p. 134; Wikipedia.org, p. 17.

Subhead Illustrations: J. G. Heck, ed., *Heck's Pictorial Archive of Military Science, Geography, and
History*, published by Dover Publications, Inc., in 1994

Cover Illustration: ©ARPL/HIP/The Image Works (Bust of Pericles, made by a Roman sculptor
sometime in the second century, B.C.)

CONTENTS

Epidamnus

N
W—E
S

Corcyra

Sybota
Islands

Delphi

Ionian
Sea

Elis
Megara
Corinth
Olympia
Argos
Mantinea
Thebes
PELOPONNESUS

Sparta

EUBOEA

Athens

ATTICA

Aegean
Sea

PERSIAN EMPIRE

Smyrna

Samos
Ephesus

Miletus

Rhodes

Sea of Crete

Mediterranean
Sea

ANCIENT GREECE DURING
PERICLES'S TIME

1

BATTLING THE SAMIANS

Pericles of Athens stood near the bow of his ship as the mountains of Samos rose out of the sea. His fleet of forty warships was fast approaching the island city-state located a few miles off the coast of Asia Minor (what is now Turkey). By Pericles' time—the mid-fifth century B.C.—western Asia Minor had already been Greek for several centuries. The Greek cities and islands that lined the coast were collectively called Ionia. The largest of the Ionian cities, Miletus, lay on the mainland of Asia Minor only a few miles southeast of Samos.

In fact, it was a dispute between Miletus and Samos that had drawn Pericles and his troops to the area. Miletus and Samos had become rivals in the eighth century B.C. Like Athens and other Greek city-states rising to prominence in those days, each was fiercely independent and viewed itself as a sovereign nation.

Both Samos and Miletus early developed strong fleets, with which they carried on vigorous trade throughout the eastern Mediterranean sphere. Early in 440 B.C., news reached Athens that the Samians and Milesians were squabbling over the possession of Priene, a city lying not far north of Miletus. A Milesian delegation came to Athens and, according to the contemporary Greek historian Thucydides, "lodged violent protests against the Samians." These ambassadors demanded that Athens take Miletus's side in the dispute. "Their cause," said Thucydides, "was supported by various private individuals from Samos itself who wished to set up there a different form of government."[1] (At the time, a council of wealthy aristocrats ruled Samos.)

HEADING FOR A MAJOR CONFRONTATION

For these reasons, in the summer of 440 B.C., Pericles gathered his forces and sailed across the Aegean Sea to Samos. At first, the island's leaders were taken off guard and offered little opposition. The Athenians came ashore and Pericles and his officers promptly dissolved the ruling aristocratic council. In its place, they installed a democratic government staffed by Samians who had long opposed the local aristocrats.

Pericles saw that many Samians did not want democracy and resented Athens's intrusion in their affairs. A number of wealthy Samians even offered him hefty cash bribes if he would take his forces and leave. But Pericles was a steadfast champion of democracy.

In his mind, Samos would be better off with a democratic government; and Athens would be better off, too, because Samian democrats would likely be more supportive of Athenian policy than Samian aristocrats.

It was clear to Pericles that some of these aristocrats might try to cause trouble for the new government. So he took a number of them hostage. He also took fifty of their children hostage. The Athenians put the hostages on a ship and took them to Lemnos, a northern Aegean island. (Like Samos, Lemnos was a member of the Delian League, an alliance of more than a hundred Greek cities and islands controlled and exploited by Athens.) The meaning of this move was clear to all involved. The safety of the hostages depended on the good behavior of the members of the anti-Athenian faction on Samos.

Confident that the Samian expedition had been a success, Pericles gathered his men and sailed back to Athens. Soon, however, he learned that he had been more than a little overconfident about the situation on Samos. Shortly after the Athenian fleet withdrew from the island, the local aristocrats launched a rebellion and retook control. It did not take long for news of these events to reach Pericles and the other Athenian leaders. It was clear to them that they could not allow the Samian rebels to defy Athens and its iron rule of the Delian League. So another Athenian fleet immediately set sail. This time, Pericles knew, he and his men were heading for a major confrontation, one in which many people on both sides would likely be killed.

SAMOS AN EARLY NAVAL POWER

Part of the reason that the Samians resisted Pericles and his troops so vigorously was that the islanders had a long and proud history of independence and naval supremacy. Samos was one of the first Greek city-states to build a large fleet of ships. In the late eighth century B.C. and throughout the century that followed, these vessels ranged far and wide. They established rich trade routes across the Mediterranean sphere. The Samians even set up their own merchant quarter at Naucratis, in Egypt.

Samos was also a leader in early exploration, as one Samian, Colaeus, sailed through the Pillars of Heracles (Strait of Gibraltar) and into the Atlantic Ocean. Further Samian naval expansion came in the 500s B.C. under a forceful autocratic leader, Polycrates, who built the capital city's deep-sea harbor. As a leading Greek naval power, Samos was bound sooner or later to face competition from Athens, which had Greece's largest war fleets by the early fifth century B.C., when Pericles was a child.

 ## ATTACK AND COUNTERATTACK

On arriving in Samian waters with forty-four ships, Pericles found a Samian war fleet of seventy ships arrayed and ready to give battle. According to Thucydides and Pericles' ancient Greek biographer, Plutarch, the Athenians won the battle. The Samian rebels remained defiant, however. Even the arrival of a second Athenian fleet did not deter them from fighting on against the greatest naval power of the day. The situation had now become a major confrontation, just as Pericles had feared it would. He knew that the entire Greek world was watching his every move. In particular, Athens's powerful rival, Sparta, would look for signs of Athenian weakness and perhaps try to exploit them.

At this point, Pericles made his second mistake in his dealings with Samos. He took sixty of his ships, comprising perhaps half or more of his forces, and sailed southward into the eastern Mediterranean. A fleet of Persian warships was on its way to help the Samian rebels. And he wanted to intercept and destroy these vessels well before they reached Samian waters. His departure once more emboldened the leading rebels. They now counterattacked, as recalled by Plutarch:

> In the battle . . . the Samians scored a victory, took a large number of Athenian prisoners and destroyed many of their ships, so that they now gained command of the sea and were enabled to lay in [collect] warlike supplies which they did not possess before. . . . The Samians . . . branded their Athenian prisoners on the forehead with an owl [the symbol of Athens's patron goddess, Athena, which also appeared on Athenian coins].[2]

The days of Samian triumph were few in number, however. Pericles soon returned with his sixty ships. After decisively defeating the Samians, the Athenians drove them back to the island's capital, also named Samos. Pericles ordered his soldiers to erect a stone wall around the landward side of the city. (Athenian ships blockaded the seaward side.) The purpose of the wall was to keep reinforcements from getting in, as well as to keep the defenders from escaping. The Athenians kept the city surrounded for nine months, until finally the Samians surrendered early in 439 B.C.

ATHENS NOT INVINCIBLE

Pericles now realized that he had to enforce harsh terms on the rebels in order to save face. The truth was that a small force of determined islanders had fought bravely against and badly embarrassed the mighty Athens. So Pericles ordered that the town's defensive walls be torn down. He also confiscated all the Samian ships and imposed heavy monetary fines on the Samians.

But as a veteran and seasoned politician, Pericles worried that this might not be enough to prevent a much larger war. He knew full well that the Spartans and their allies had been watching. They had paid close attention to the difficulty with which the Athenians had overcome the Samians. In short, Athens had revealed that it was not invincible. And this might embolden the Spartans and their allies to resist the Athenians on a wider front. As it turned out, history was about to transform the Athenian leader's worries into reality. Soon, the whole Greek world would be engulfed in a devastating, bloody war in which Pericles himself would meet his end in a completely unexpected and quite horrifying way.

2

BORN IN A PIVOTAL TIME

The extraordinary man who presided over ancient Athens's brief but glorious cultural golden age was born in about 495 B.C. Pericles belonged to the prestigious Alcmaeonid clan. Like other Greek cities, Athens had strong tribal roots, each local tribe being an extended kinship group in which everyone was related to one degree or another. In turn, each tribe broke down into several clans. A fairly close-knit group, a typical clan was composed of a handful of individual families. The Alcmaeonids had been prominent in Athens for a long time. In the seventh century B.C., a distant ancestor, Megacles, had been archon (a leading city administrator). And circa 592 B.C., his son, Alcmaeon, had won Athens's first victory in chariot racing at the Olympic Games.

It was Pericles' mother, Agariste, who provided his connection to the powerful Alcmaeonids. Her uncle,

Cleisthenes, had recently (in 508 B.C.) led the social and political revolution that had brought democracy to Athens. Thus, Pericles was not only born into wealth and privilege. He was also a member of one of the leading families of the city's most democratic faction. (Other factions advocated less open forms of democracy or felt a ruling council of aristocrats would be better.) Thus it is no wonder that he grew up believing that democracy was by far the best form of government and championed it at every turn. Young Pericles also had close ties with the military leadership through his father, Xanthippus. A member of another prominent Athenian clan, Xanthippus eventually became a *strategos* (general) and military hero.

As in the cases of so many other notable people of ancient times, rumors and fables about Pericles' birth arose after his death. According to folk beliefs, certain individuals were somehow chosen for greatness by the gods or fate and that signs of this greatness were forecast at birth. Supposedly, while she was pregnant, Agariste had a vivid dream in which she gave birth to a handsome and powerful lion. Soon after the dream, she had Pericles. To the ancients, lions were potent symbols of strength and bravery, hence the foreshadowing of the child's future greatness.

Whether or not Pericles' mother ever had such a dream, he did turn out to be quite handsome. A number of short passages in the ancient sources mention his good looks and imposing stature. He did have one physical drawback, however, as Plutarch wrote:

Pericles' father, Xanthippus (seated), was an Athenian naval commander.

His physical features were almost perfect, the only exception being his head, which was rather long and out of proportion. For this reason, all of his portraits show him wearing a helmet, since the artists apparently did not wish to taunt him with his deformity. However, the comic poets of Athens nicknamed him "schinocephalus," or "squill-head." [A squill is a bulbous sea onion.][1]

A YOUTH SHAPED BY EPIC EVENTS

No stories that described how Pericles dealt with taunts about his head delivered by his young playmates have survived. In fact, almost nothing specific is known about his childhood. However, the social and political conditions and events of Pericles' early days are known. It is possible, therefore, to trace the epic events he witnessed and took part in, occurrences that helped shape his character and outlook on life and politics.

It is now clear that Pericles was born in a pivotal place and time in the saga of Western civilization. When he was about four, the first Persian attack on Greece took place. The Persian Empire, centered in what are now Iraq and Iran, was the largest and most powerful realm on Earth. In the previous century, the Persians had seized control of most of the Ionian Greek cities on the other side of the Aegean Sea. Then, in 499 B.C., the Ionians had rebelled against their Persian overlords. The insurrection eventually ended in failure. However, while it was in full swing Athens had sent ships and soldiers to help the rebels. The Persian king, Darius I, never forgot that Athens had dared to interfere in his affairs. So in 490 B.C., he sent an army to punish the Greek city. (He also wanted to establish a military foothold in Greece from which to launch a larger invasion of Europe.)

The intrepid Athenians marshaled their army. (Its members were militiamen—farmers who grabbed weapons during an emergency and returned to their farms when the fighting was over.) Though greatly outnumbered, the Greek troops crushed the invaders on the plain of Marathon (about twenty-five miles northeast of Athens). It is almost certain that Xanthippus fought in the battle. His wife, Agariste, and young son, Pericles, took part in the huge celebration held in the city following the victory. In the years that followed, Pericles must have sat enraptured as his father and other veterans—the so-called Men of Marathon—told and retold stories of their exploits against the "barbarians." (This was the term that Greeks customarily, and rather arrogantly, used to describe non-Greeks.)

For both Xanthippus and Pericles, however, the glory of the victory at Marathon had been marred by an unfortunate incident. After their defeat, the Persians sailed around the Attic peninsula in hopes of attacking Athens before the Athenian troops had had a chance to

THE PERSIAN KING'S HATRED FOR ATHENS

On hearing that the Athenians had aided the Ionians in the rebellion they staged in the 490s B.C., Persia's King Darius I vowed to achieve vengeance on Athens. According to the fifth century B.C. Greek historian Herodotus in his Histories:

> He did not give a thought to the Ionians, knowing perfectly well that the punishment for their revolt would come. But he asked who the Athenians were, and then, on being told, called for his bow. He took it, set an arrow on the string, shot it up into the air and cried: "Grant, O God, that I may punish the Athenians." Then he commanded one of his servants to repeat to him the words, "Master, remember the Athenians," three times, whenever he sat down to dinner.[2]

make it home. According to the fifth-century B.C. Greek historian Herodotus, "The Alcmaeonids were accused of suggesting this move. They had, it was said, an understanding with the Persians, and raised a shield [to reflect the sun's light] as a signal to them when they were already on board [their ships]."[3]

The Family Name Blackened

These charges of treachery leveled against Pericles' clan were probably false. As Pericles' noted modern biographer, Donald Kagan, suggests, they were likely "invented by their political enemies, eager to put an end to the strong position the Alcmaeonids and their associates had held since the revolution of Cleisthenes."[4] Still, for a time, these charges blackened the family name. And Pericles no doubt found himself shunned by some of his childhood friends.

In addition, Xanthippus regularly faced off against political enemies, who continued their attempts to discredit the family. These efforts ended in 484 B.C. with Xanthippus's ostracism. Ostracism was one of Athens's recently acquired democratic processes. It had been installed partly to prevent one leader from amassing too much power. It was also intended as a form of impeachment, a way to get rid of a leader whose policies seemed to impede the democratic decision-making process. The Athenians voted each year on whether or not to have an ostracism. If they decided it was necessary, the citizens convened in the early spring. Each voter took a piece of broken pottery, called an ostrakon, and scratched on it the name of the politician he wanted to remove from office. The leader who received the most votes (provided that a minimum of six thousand votes were cast) was banished from Athens for ten years. (However, he did not lose his citizenship or property.)

One negative aspect of ostracism was that it could be used by one political party to silence or cripple an opposing party. This is what happened to Pericles' father. Xanthippus's enemies were able to muster enough voters to order his banishment. Per custom, his family accompanied him in his exile. That meant that Pericles, then about ten years old, suddenly had to leave his boyhood home. The family's destination is unknown. But it may have been Sicyon (about fifty miles west of Athens), where Agariste had distant relatives.

THE SECOND PERSIAN INVASION

The family's forced exile must have made a strong impression on young Pericles. He was certainly old enough to know what was happening. And as Kagan points out, the boy "doubtless drew from [the experience] an early and vivid lesson of the dangers attending the competition for political power."[5]

One positive aspect of the exile was that it was unexpectedly short. Less than four years after Xanthippus was banished, the Persians made their second and largest foray into Greece. Thrown into a state of national emergency, the Athenians recalled all of their citizens, including those in exile, to defend their country.

The momentous events of this war forever and dramatically changed the fate of Athens and its leading citizens, including Pericles. King Darius had died in the mid-480s B.C. before he could fulfill his vengeance against Athens for the embarrassment of Marathon. But his son, Xerxes (ZERK-seez), eagerly carried forward his father's war plans. At the head of the largest invasion force assembled anywhere in the world in ancient times, Xerxes marched around the Aegean's northern rim and descended into mainland Greece in 480 B.C.

At age fourteen or fifteen, Pericles was too young to fight. (The minimum age was eighteen.) But there were many other war-related tasks for able-bodied young men to perform. Perhaps the single most important was helping to evacuate Athens's urban center, which sprawled around the rocky Acropolis. As the Persian horde approached the city, the leading general, Themistocles, ordered the people to move to a safer position about forty miles to the southwest. The Persians soon entered the deserted city. But they, too, were forced to evacuate. On or about September 20, 480 B.C. Themistocles decisively defeated them in a huge naval battle fought in the Salamis Strait, six miles west of the Acropolis.

Meanwhile, Pericles' father was given the post of general. The following summer (August 479 B.C.), he led the Athenian contingent of a united Greek army that crossed the Aegean. At Mycale, not far from the island of Samos, the Greeks assaulted a large enemy force. Almost all of the Persians were killed. And Xanthippus returned to Greece with a completely refurbished reputation. He and his family, including Pericles, were back in Athens to stay.

THE BEST EDUCATION AVAILABLE

The fight at Mycale was the last battle of the war. A handful of small independent Greek city-states had driven away and humbled the most powerful empire on Earth. Themistocles, Xanthippus, Pericles, and other members of leading Athenian families benefited most from the victory. This is because Athens had played a major role in the resistance against the Persians. Along with Sparta (which possessed the strongest land army in Greece), Athens now emerged as one of Greece's two most influential states. In the years that followed, Athens expanded its trade routes far and wide and became increasingly prosperous. It also took the political lead in Greek affairs by organizing the Delian League (the alliance intended to guard against further Persian incursions).

In the face of all this prosperity, Pericles' already wealthy family grew even richer. This meant that the young man could afford the best education available. Nothing specific is known about his elementary classes. But it is likely that he received the same basic early education that most middle-and upper-class Athenian boys did. First, young boys (and girls, too) learned a great deal about life from listening to their parents, grandparents, and other relatives tell stories. Some were traditional tales about the history of their city-state or

21

myths about famous gods and human heroes of the distant past. Other stories recalled the past exploits or difficulties of specific family or clan members. Whatever the nature of the story, a child learned what society and life in general expected of them and the difference between right and wrong.

Like other Athenian boys, at about the age of seven or eight Pericles probably began attending a formal grammar school. (Girls generally did not attend school and learned household arts from their mothers instead.) No public schools existed. Rather, parents paid the teachers, who taught the students reading and writing skills. Having learned to read, Pericles began absorbing and memorizing long passages by renowned Greek poets. The Athenian philosopher Plato (who lived in the century following the Periclean age) commented, "In these [works] are contained many pieces of advice, and many tales, and praises and glorification of ancient famous men, which [the student] is required to learn by heart, in order that he may imitate . . . and desire to become like them."[6]

Among the works the boys studied, the most revered were two epic poems by the eighth-century B.C. bard Homer. *The Iliad* described the legendary Trojan War. *The Odyssey* told about the adventures of the hero Odysseus in the years following that war. These poems were (and still are) widely seen as the pinnacle of Greek literature, and Pericles and other Greek boys drew many religious, moral, and life lessons from them.

It is also probable that Pericles' parents followed custom and had a *paidagogos* accompany him to school.

Usually a male slave, the paidagogos kept an eye on the boy, made sure he behaved himself, and disciplined him if necessary. Such discipline might include corporal punishment, which was common in ancient Greece. A few whacks with a rod or switch by the paidagogos was usually enough to prevent the boy from continuing to be lazy or disobedient.

Higher education began in a boy's teen years. The teachers were paid tutors who provided mainly athletic, musical, and philosophical training. "Physical activity, both musical and gymnastic," Kagan explains,

> taught competitiveness and courage, moderation, harmony and self-control. At its core was the idea that education should shape an individual's body and character to make him fit to take his place in the community. The aristocratic ideal was of a talented amateur exercising a variety of skills but achieving a professional mastery of none.[7]

Among Pericles' distinguished teachers was Damon, an Athenian, who instructed the young man in music. Actually, Pericles seems to have learned more than just music from Damon. "This Damon," Plutarch wrote, "used his musical teaching as a screen to conceal his real talents from the world in general. In fact, it was he who trained Pericles for his political contests."[8]

LEARNING TO TRUST IN THE RATIONAL

However, it was Anaxagoras, a thinker and teacher who hailed from the Ionian city of Clazomenae, who most shaped Pericles' ideas about politics and life in general. Anaxagoras was a metic. This was the Athenian term for a foreigner (either a Greek from another city or a non-Greek) who lived in Athens. Metics were not citizens and so lacked many civic rights (including attending and voting in the Assembly). Also, their social status was below that of citizens (free people born in Athens).

Yet, Anaxagoras was widely respected, even in aristocratic circles. His nickname was "Intelligence Personified," earned for what Plutarch described as "the extraordinary intellectual powers he displayed in the investigation of natural phenomena."[9] Thus, Anaxagoras was a noted philosopher-scientist. (Philosophy and science, both pioneered by the Greeks, had not yet become separate disciplines.)

Soon Pericles and Anaxagoras were more than simply teacher and student. They became close friends. From the older man, the younger learned many useful skills he would put to effective use later in life. In particular, Anaxagoras taught Pericles how to bear himself with dignity in public and to deliver speeches with authority and conviction.

From their sessions together, Plutarch recalled that Pericles

> derived not only a dignity of spirit and a nobility of utterance [speaking] . . . but also a composure . . . a serenity [calmness] in his movements and in the graceful arrangement of his dress . . . a firm and evenly modulated voice, and other characteristics . . . which deeply impressed [Pericles' future] audiences.[10]

In addition to young Pericles, Anaxagoras also taught the Greek playwright Euripides.

Anaxagoras also freed Pericles from fears that sprang from a wide range of superstitions that were common in ancient times. Like most other Greek philosopher-scientists, Anaxagoras taught that the wonders of nature are not magical and beyond human understanding. Rather, they result from physical processes that people can ultimately discover and explain. In particular, he stressed the importance of the mind and its unique perceptive powers, which he held separate from other aspects of nature. "Mind is unlimited, autonomous, and unmixed with anything, standing entirely by itself," a surviving fragment of his writings states. "The truth is that Mind, because of its exceptional fineness and purity, has knowledge of all that is, and therein it has the greatest power."[11]

Thus, Anaxagoras taught Pericles to seek, or at least trust in the existence of, rational explanations for all that happens. In this way, the younger man learned to disregard superstition and ignorant fears of unexplained natural events.

Tolerance in the Face of Abuse

Among the many admirable abilities Pericles learned from Anaxagoras were tolerance for others' opinions and the ability to control his temper, no matter how much a situation or person might irritate him. As he grew older, Pericles also came to believe that it was the right of every citizen in a democratic society to exercise free speech against the government and its leaders. These facets of his character explain his conduct in a potentially volatile situation that occurred when he was a leading general. Plutarch recorded the incident in his biography of Pericles:

> Once in the marketplace, where he had urgent business to transact, he allowed himself to be abused and reviled for an entire day by some idle hooligan without uttering a word in reply. Towards evening he returned home unperturbed, while the man followed close behind, still heaping every kind of insult upon him. When Pericles was about to go indoors, as it was now dark, he ordered one of his servants to take a torch and escort the man all the way to his own house.[12]

Unique Experiences and Unconventional Ideas

Pericles took these ideas to heart and in later years applied them to real-life situations. This is proven by an incident that occurred during the years when he was commanding troops in wartime. Just as his fleet of ships was about to embark on a crucial campaign, an eclipse of the sun occurred. As darkness descended on the land and sea alike, many of the troops began to panic. They automatically accepted the traditional view that an eclipse was an evil omen—a sign sent by a god or gods to warn of a coming disaster. "When Pericles saw that his helmsman was frightened and quite at a loss [about] what to do," Plutarch wrote, Pericles held up his cloak in front of the man's eyes and asked him whether he found this alarming or thought it a terrible omen. When he replied that he did not, Pericles asked, "What is the difference, then, between this and the eclipse,

A bust of Pericles in adulthood

except that the eclipse has been caused by something bigger than my cloak?"[13]

Pericles was therefore no exception to the rule that much of what a grown person thinks and does is shaped by the events of his or her childhood. His future greatness was to some degree primed by a unique and unusual series of early experiences. He was born into wealth; exposed to the inner workings of power politics; a witness to war and human strife on a grand scale; and in direct contact with some of the greatest minds of his day. The last of these may well have been the most important. As Kagan suggests:

> His extraordinary intellectual training and the philosophical vision that arose from it transcended [rose above] the general outlook of his peers and shaped his policies throughout this career. . . . Like other aristocrats, he sought the victory, recognition, and glory that came with political success. Unlike the others, however, he brought to the battle unconventional ideas of greatness for his city and of the possibilities for political leadership.[14]

3

VYING FOR POLITICAL POWER

For a young man who clearly had political aspirations, Pericles at first kept a surprisingly low public profile. As Plutarch put it, he was "inclined to shrink from facing the people." One reason Plutarch cites for this is that Pericles bore a striking resemblance to Pisistratus, a man who had ruled Athens as a tyrant in the preceding century. Evidently the younger man was afraid that some people might associate him with the former dictatorship. Another reason that Pericles was reluctant at first to throw himself fully into the political ring was his wealth. "The fact that he was rich," Plutarch wrote, "and that he came from a distinguished family and possessed exceedingly powerful friends made the fear of ostracism very real to him."[1] Indeed, as Pericles entered his twenties (in the mid-470s B.C.), the memory of his father's ostracism and banishment must still have been fresh in his mind.

However, the main reason for Pericles' initial low political profile was undoubtedly the strength of his competition. When he was in his late teens and early twenties, the Athenian political scene was dominated by a few very popular men. One was Aristides, often referred to as Aristides "the just." Renowned for his honesty and fairness, he had been a general in the Persian conflicts. Another powerful politician, Themistocles, had engineered Athens's emergence as a great naval power. He had also won the great sea battle of Salamis, a victory that had forced Persia's King Xerxes to retreat to Asia Minor.

Finally, there was Cimon, son of Miltiades, the Athenian general who had led the victory at Marathon. Cimon was young, good-looking, and the darling of the old but still influential aristocratic class. Ultimately, Cimon constituted the biggest obstacle to Pericles' rise to political power. To confront and hopefully remove that obstacle, Pericles realized, would require opposing the nobles and backing the commoners. And this was a calculated risk. After all, he was himself a member of the wealthy aristocratic set. But he was willing to take that risk to advance his career and for what he viewed as the ultimate good of his native city.

THE RISE OF CIMON

In examining this political rivalry between Pericles and Cimon, it is important to understand what Plutarch and other ancient writers meant by the term "parties." No modern-style political parties existed in Athens and other Greek cities. There were no party platforms, nominating conventions, or organized political campaigns. Instead, politics in Athens's democracy was dominated by a handful of strong individuals. Each gathered around him a faction—a hard-core group of supporters. As Donald Kagan explains:

> The ancient writers referred to such factions as "those around Themistocles" or "Cimon and his friends.". . . The formation of such a group required first and foremost a leader who could attract a following. All political leaders in Pericles' early years were aristocrats and almost all were rich. The core of their political groups was typically formed by their relatives, their friends, and those dependent on or influenced by these people. To go beyond that circle, a political leader needed special personal qualities and achievements.[2]

Pericles certainly possessed a number of such special personal qualities. He was good-looking, shrewd, and an excellent public speaker. (Good oratory skills were particularly important because politicians had to stand and speak in the Assembly; this was the principal means of winning the support of the voters.) But as Pericles well knew, his main opponent, Cimon, also had many admirable qualities and talents. "He was as brave as Miltiades and as intelligent as Themistocles," Plutarch wrote.

> And he is generally admitted to have been a juster man than either. . . . And in statesmanship he showed himself immeasurably their superior, even when he was quite young. . . . His physical presence was imposing, too . . .

for he was tall with a thick and curly head of hair. And as he proved himself a brilliant and courageous soldier in the battle of Salamis, he quickly won not only the praise but also the hearts of his countrymen. . . . So when he first entered politics, the Athenians welcomed him gladly.[3]

The young Pericles quietly watched as Cimon divided the chief elder statesmen of the day—Aristides and Themistocles. Aristides backed Cimon. But Themistocles increasingly opposed Cimon, especially over policies relating to Sparta. As a champion of naval power, Themistocles saw that Athens's destiny lay in building and utilizing large fleets of ships. He therefore strongly advocated the ambitious policy of creating and shaping the emerging Delian League.

In contrast, the Spartans did not have a large navy. They were also very conservative, both socially and politically. The Spartans distrusted Athenian democracy, seeing it as unstable, and considered ambitious democrats like Themistocles to be dangerous men. It is not surprising, therefore, that Themistocles became openly anti-Spartan in both his speeches and actions. Pericles, too, took this anti-Spartan position, although for the moment he apparently kept his feelings to himself.

Meanwhile, Cimon took advantage of Spartan dislike for Themistocles. Cimon did play an active role in the formation of the Delian League. And he led a number of expeditions against lingering Persian forces in Asia Minor. But at home he led Athens's pro-Spartan party, which was made up almost exclusively of aristocrats. In his view, rather than be enemies, Athens and

Sparta should maintain the unity they had recently shown against the invading Persians. For a time, a majority of Athenian voters accepted this view. Cimon eventually managed to discredit Themistocles in their eyes. And in about 473 or 472 B.C., Themistocles was ostracized and banished. This left Cimon and the conservative, pro-Spartan party in power in Athens.

THE BASICS OF ATHENIAN DEMOCRACY

Pericles must have been more than a little upset by the success of Cimon and the aristocrats. On the one hand, Pericles distrusted the Spartans, as Themistocles had. It was clear to Athenians like Pericles that Sparta hoped to take advantage of its good relations with Cimon to reign in and blunt Athenian power and expansion.

Pericles and his own supporters also disliked the limitations that Cimon and the aristocrats placed on Athenian democracy. At the time of Themistocles' ostracism, the city's democratic government was only a little more than thirty years old. Cleisthenes, who had established the democracy, had been an aristocrat. And almost all of the political leaders who had succeeded him had been aristocrats, too. True, most of these upper-class individuals supported the basic concept of democracy; however, they still believed that the aristocrats knew what was best for the state and society. So they were reluctant to cede too much power to the common citizenry.

THE ARCHONS UNDER DEMOCRACY

City administrators called *archons* (arkhontes) existed in Athens in the seventh century B.C. and probably even earlier. For a long time, they were aristocrats chosen by the leading citizens. And after leaving office, each archon became a lifetime member of the city's aristocratic council—the Areopagus, which advised the archons. After the introduction of democracy in Athens, the archons were retained, but the method for choosing them, as well as some of their functions, changed. Beginning in 487 B.C., they were chosen by lot (random drawing).

The archon known as the *polemarch* had originally been the commander in chief of the army; but under the democracy this duty was assigned to the ten generals, and the polemarch became a civilian official in charge of lawsuits involving foreigners. In the distant past, the so-called king archon had assumed the duties of Athens's kings after the kingship was abolished. Under the democracy, the king archon supervised the community's religious functions. There was also an eponymous archon, who dealt with state festivals and family matters, and six *thesmothetai* ("keepers of the law"), who supervised the law courts. In Athens's democracy, archons served for one year and were not eligible for reelection.

In fact, Cimon and his supporters likely thought the commoners already possessed too much say in government. In theory, for instance, any male member of the citizen body, or demos, could attend meetings of the Assembly. (Free women born in Athens were citizens, too. But unlike men, they had no political rights and could not attend the Assembly.) In such meetings, the citizens did more than simply elect some of the public officials. They also declared war, made peace, formed commercial alliances, established colonies, and decided state foreign policy.

The Assembly worked closely with another pivotal democratic institution—the *Boule*, or Council. The five hundred members of the Council were chosen by lot (random drawing) and served for one year. They prepared the Assembly's agenda by drafting legislative bills (called *probouleumata*) dealing with state business and the community in general. The citizens who met in the Assembly debated and voted on these bills, which might or might not pass. Sometimes a bill that did not pass was sent back to the Council to be revised.

Another job of the Council was to ensure that the Assembly's laws, decisions, and orders were carried out. To accomplish this, the councilors set up a series of subcommittees (boards of councilors), which closely supervised the work of nine public officials known as archons. The noted fourth-century B.C. Athenian scholar and philosopher Aristotle described such a subcommittee in action:

35

The Council also inspects triremes [warships] after construction, and their rigging, and the naval shed, and has new triremes . . . voted for by the Assembly, built and rigged, and naval sheds built; but naval architects are elected by the Assembly. . . . For the building of the triremes it [the Council] elects ten of its own members as Naval Constructors. It also inspects all public buildings, and if it finds any commissioner in default, it reports him to the Assembly, and if it gets a verdict of guilty hands him over to a jury-court.[4]

ARISTOCRATIC CHECKS ON THE COMMON PEOPLE

Pericles was well aware that in theory these democratic powers of the Assembly and Council gave the common people a great deal of authority. But he also knew that the aristocrats who had founded the democracy and still largely controlled it had been careful not to let that authority go unchecked. One way the common people's powers were limited, at least at first, was through the workings of the *Strategia*, the board of ten generals (*strategoi*). These men were elected by the Assembly. But in the early fifth century B.C., they were almost always aristocrats. This is because aristocrats tended to be the best educated and the most accomplished speakers. They also had enough money and time to get the support of the various groups of the public.

In addition, the generals were not subject to term limits, as councilors and archons were. (Usually the multiple one-year terms of councilors and archons could not be served consecutively.) A strategos could serve an unlimited number of consecutive terms as long as the people kept reelecting him. The generals also had the power to call meetings of the Assembly and to create or sponsor legislation. This meant that a handful of very powerful men, most of them aristocrats, swayed many of the Assembly's decisions and carried out all state foreign policy. Therefore, a popular general could be and often was the most influential and powerful member of the community. (One limit placed on that power, of course, was the process of ostracism.)

An even stronger check on the authority of the Assembly and commoners consisted of the Areopagus. This was an ancient aristocratic council that had been the center of Athens's pre-democratic government. Its members met on a low hill of the same name lying not far from the Acropolis. They were all ex-public officials. For centuries they had been aristocrats who served in the Areopagus for life and closely advised the archons and other state officials.

In Pericles' early years, both the board of generals and Areopagus had been undergoing change. The longer democracy was in place, the more non-aristocrats became members of both institutions. Those Athenians who supported radical democracy (rule of the people without aristocratic restraints) wanted to speed this process up. They especially wanted to reduce the powers and influence of the Areopagus. Themistocles had long been the leader of this group. After his removal, others took his place, among them an active democratic reformer named Ephialtes. Pericles, who found himself increasingly in agreement with the radicals, soon became Ephialtes' close associate.

PERICLES AND AESCHYLUS

However, the radical democrats realized that the time was not yet right to make their move against the Areopagus. Cimon and his aristocratic supporters still had too strong a hold on the Assembly. Ephialtes and Pericles calculated that they could not yet get the votes needed to break the power of the nobles.

For the time being, therefore, Pericles concentrated on increasing his own popularity with the general populace. True to his character, he did so in a low-key manner. In fact, he was very careful to avoid the blatant sort of pandering in which Cimon engaged. According to Plutarch, Cimon "provided a dinner at his house every day, a simple meal but enough for large numbers. Any poor man who wished could come to him for this."[5]

In contrast, Pericles chose a more indirect way to gain popularity. This was to use his wealth to back well-attended public events and functions. In so doing, he took advantage of a series of public services known as liturgies, which democratic politicians saw as a way to win public support. Liturgies consisted of wealthy individuals spending their money and time to sponsor public activities. One could maintain a warship and train its crew or pay for a feast held during a religious festival or pay for the training of choruses for Athens's dramatic contests.

The backers of the choruses for plays were known as *choregoi*. Each year the chief archon chose three playwrights to present their works in the local Theater of Dionysus (located at the base of the Acropolis). He also selected a well-to-do choregus for each playwright. The yearly dramatic competition, in which a prize was given for the best playwright, was widely popular. All of the participants, including playwrights, actors, and backers, gained in notoriety and prestige.

In 472 B.C. Pericles became choregus for the playwright Aeschylus (today recognized as one of the world's first great dramatists). Aeschylus presented four plays, one of which has survived. Titled *The Persians*, it describes the great Greek victory over the Persians in the sea battle of Salamis. (Aeschylus fought in the battle himself, as well as in the earlier battle of Marathon.) It should be noted that staging a play about Salamis at that particular point in time made a strong political statement. The victory had been engineered by Themistocles, a radical democrat who had recently been banished. Presenting the play made it clear to those who had ostracized Themistocles that his political causes were still very much alive. In fact, this message came through loudly when Aeschylus and Pericles won the competition.

PERICLES AND EPHIALTES MAKE THEIR MOVE

After this triumph, Pericles decided to continue building his reputation in a completely different way. He saw that

39

REMEMBERING THE VICTORY AT SALAMIS

When Pericles backed Aeschylus's play, *The Persians*, in 472 B.C., he knew full well that to some degree he was making a political statement. Theatergoers would be reminded of the heroism of the victor of the battle of Salamis—Themistocles. Aeschylus's eyewitness account of the battle is excerpted in this passage (Philip Vellacott's translation), in which a Persian messenger describes the carnage to the Persian king's mother:

> A [Greek] ship charged first and chopped off the whole stern of a [Persian] galley. Then charge followed charge on every side. . . . Soon, in that narrow space, our ships were jammed in hundreds; none could help another. They rammed each other . . . and some were stripped of every oar. Meanwhile the enemy came round us in a ring and charged. Our vessels heeled over; the sea was hidden, carpeted with wrecks and dead men; all the shores and reefs were full of dead. Then every ship we had broke rank and rowed for life. The [Greeks] seized fragments of wrecks and broken oars and hacked and stabbed at our men swimming in the sea. . . . The whole sea was one din of shrieks and dying groans, till night and darkness hid the scene.[6]

men like Cimon, Themistocles, and Pericles' own father, Xanthippus, had made names for themselves through distinguished military service. It seemed the appropriate time for Pericles to do the same. From about 472 to 466 B.C., therefore, he took part in a number of military expeditions. Most of these appear to have consisted of raids by Delian League members on Persian interests in southern Asia Minor. In these endeavors, Pericles handily fulfilled his goal of making a name for himself. In 465 B.C., he was elected strategos for the first time.

That year was noteworthy as a turning point in other ways as well. Ephialtes, too, was elected general. And Cimon launched an attack on Thasos, the northernmost Aegean island and member of the Delian League. The Thasians claimed that they owned a gold mine located nearby. Cimon wanted the gold for Athens and brazenly laid siege to the island.

Cimon's expedition against Thasos became increasingly unpopular in Athens. Ephialtes and Pericles sensed that the time had come to make their move against the leader of the aristocratic faction. While Cimon was still mired down on Thasos, in Athens the radical democrats launched political attacks on members of the Areopagus. Then, when Cimon returned to Athens in 463 B.C., Ephialtes, Pericles, and their associates brought him to trial. They accused him of mismanaging the Thasos affair. But more importantly, they charged him with taking bribes from the leaders of another Greek state. Pericles himself was one of the prosecutors in the trial.

THE FALL OF CIMON

Very few details of Cimon's trial have survived. What is certain is that his opponents were unable to make any of the charges stick and he was acquitted. Ephialtes and Pericles did not give up, however. Only a few months later, another political crisis arose that gave them fresh ammunition against Cimon.

The pivotal series of events leading to this crisis began in 464 B.C., when Cimon was in the midst of laying siege to Thasos. A disastrous earthquake had struck Sparta, leveling almost every house. Taking advantage of the situation, the Spartan serfs, called *helots*, who had long been badly mistreated, rebelled. Faced with this double calamity, the Spartan government and army were strained to the limit. Early in 462, Spartan leaders swallowed their pride and requested Athenian aid.

Athens's political factions were deeply divided about how to react to the Spartans' request. Ephialtes and Pericles opposed it. They pleaded with the Athenians not to send aid to a city that everyone acknowledged to be Athens's greatest rival. However, Cimon argued for helping the Spartans and managed to convince the members of the Assembly to send a large group of Athenian soldiers to Sparta.

To Cimon's everlasting regret, however, these soldiers had a rude awakening when they reached Sparta. For reasons unknown, the Spartan leaders curtly informed the rescuers that they were not needed and that they should leave Spartan territory immediately. Athenians of all classes and factions viewed this as a

In a democratic vote, the citizens of Athens ostracized Cimon.

serious insult to their national pride. Ephialtes and Pericles swiftly denounced Cimon in the Assembly. And early in 461 B.C., the citizenry ostracized Cimon. Moreover, his aristocratic supporters now found themselves pushed to the political margins.

A MOMENTOUS CHANGING OF THE GUARD

Filling the power vacuum that had been created, the radical democrats next made an all-out political assault on the Areopagus. They proposed bills that greatly limited its powers. In the space of only a few months, in fact, the old aristocratic council had been reduced to little more than a court for hearing major murder cases.

The radical democrats loudly celebrated their victory, which seemed to open the way for still more democratic reforms. However, an unexpected tragedy marred the festivities. Ephialtes was suddenly assassinated, one of only a handful of political murders recorded in Athens's long history. The killer was never positively identified. But most people suspected he had followed the orders of aristocrats who were upset over their recent loss of power.

In the long run, the most important outcome of Ephialtes' death was what it did for Pericles' career. Pericles, now about thirty-four, took his mentor's place as leader of the radical democrats. As history has shown, it turned out to be a momentous changing of the guard. On the one hand, by a stroke of good fortune, Pericles' rise to political power came in the right place at the right time. On the other, he possessed all the essential qualities needed to expand his city's democracy and lead Athens to greatness.

4

ENORMOUS AMBITIONS IN ATHENS

In the century following Pericles' lifetime, the Athenians and many other Greeks began looking back fondly and longingly at his era. In particular, they singled out a period of roughly five decades, lasting from the defeat of the Persians in 479 B.C. to Pericles' death in 429 B.C. It came to be called the *Pentekontaetia*, or the Fifty Years.

To be sure, Athens made large and important strides in the first twenty years of this period. It was instrumental in forming the Delian League. And it spread its influence and trading network far and wide. But it was the phase under Pericles' leadership, the last thirty years of the Pentekontaetia, in which Athens reached its political and cultural height. The city's democracy became one of the purest and most open in history. And in an amazingly short span of time the Athenians produced art, architecture, and literature that have awed people ever since. "Great as Athens had been when [Pericles] became her leader," Plutarch later wrote, "he made her the greatest and richest of all cities."[1]

However, one must be careful not to overemphasize the glamorous aspects of the Periclean Age, as modern scholars have come to call it. Plutarch also remarked that Pericles "came to hold more power in his hands than many a king and tyrant."[2] Indeed, more than anything else, the Fifty Years was dominated by Athens's acquisition, use, and at times abuse of great power. The Athenians displayed enormous national energies and ambitions that made other Greeks nervous and uneasy. In particular, Sparta and its own allies worried that the balance of power in Greece would be upset. As a result, relations between Athens and Sparta steadily worsened; and disputes occasionally flared up into open warfare. Modern scholars sometimes collectively call these generally minor skirmishes the "First Peloponnesian War" (in reference to the Peloponnesian War, the much larger conflict of that name that began at the conclusion of the Fifty Years).

PERICLES' LEADERSHIP STYLE

It is only natural to ask how it was that Pericles managed to maintain his popularity and power among the Athenian people for more than half of the Fifty Years. After all, he was not a dictator with access to a personal army to enforce his will on the people. Rather, he was an elected official in an open, progressive democracy. Moreover, each of his terms as general lasted only a year, by itself not enough time to consolidate much power. The key, of course, was that he managed to get reelected over and over again. Even in the few intermittent years in which he was not one of the ten generals, his influence and policies were still very much in effect. People came to see him as the city's elder statesman, the leader against whom all others were inevitably measured.

It must be emphasized that not all Athenians idolized Pericles or backed his policies. He always had

THE TACTICS OF A WISE PHYSICIAN

According to Plutarch in his biography of Pericles, that famous Athenian leader possessed an ability to sense what was best for the people and to guide them in a certain direction even when they thought it might not be the right one.

> [He struck a] firm, high note of an aristocratic, even regal statesmanship. And since he used his authority honestly and unswervingly in the interests of the city, he was usually able to carry the interests of the people with him by rational argument and persuasion. Still there were times when they bitterly resented his policy, and then he tightened the reins and forced them to do what was to their advantage, much as a wise physician treats a prolonged and complicated disease, allowing the patient at some moments pleasures which can do him no harm, and at others giving him caustics and bitter drugs which cure him.[3]

political enemies who envied him and wanted to bring him down. Like the Spartans, some Athenians thought too much democracy—that is, too much power in the hands of the common people—was dangerous. Pericles' opponents certainly felt that he personally wielded too much power. The truth is that they envied his ability to convince the people to grant him great power and then to hold onto that power by maintaining their trust and affection.

What did so many of the voters see in Pericles that inspired this trust and admiration? First, he developed a reputation for impeccable honesty early in his adult life, a quality rare in politicians in any age. "During the whole of" his career as general, Plutarch wrote, "he proved himself completely incorruptible by bribery."[4]

Second, Pericles was ever careful to maintain a discreet, modest, and completely professional profile and personal manner in his private life. As Plutarch put it:

> He was never to be seen walking in any street except the one that led to the marketplace and the Council chamber. He refused not only invitations to dinner but every kind of friendly or familiar [conversation], so that through all the years of his political career, he never visited one of his friends to dine.[5]

In marked contrast to his private life, however, Pericles was both robust and authoritative in his public life. In particular, he excelled at public speaking, which often convinced a majority of the people to back his policies. "He far excelled all other speakers," Plutarch said,

> This was the reason, some people say, for his being nicknamed "the Olympian" [a reference to the gods]. . . . They referred to him as thunder and lightning when he addressed his audience and as wielding a terrible thunderbolt in his tongue. . . . [One] political opponent of Pericles [remarked] "Whenever I throw him at wrestling, he beats me by arguing that he was never down, and he can even make the spectators believe it!"[6]

FROM ALLIANCE TO EMPIRE

These and other personal qualities explain why Pericles was able to dominate Athenian politics for so long. In theory, of course, each of the other nine generals who served alongside him held equal individual authority. His colleagues recognized the close relationship he shared with the people, however. And some of the generals were themselves awed by him. So they frequently deferred to his judgment, allowed him to speak for them, or quietly backed his bills and policies.

There was certainly very little argument among the generals about Athenian relations with other members of the Delian League. This was one area in which the aristocratic and democratic factions fundamentally agreed. Like Themistocles and Cimon before them, Pericles and his cohorts placed Athenian interests ahead of those of neighboring Greek states. These included the allies making up the Delian League. In 469 B.C., the

Aegean island of Naxos had been the first member state to feel Athens's wrath. Believing the Persian threat to be basically over, the Naxians seceded from the Delian League. Responding as though this move constituted a rebellion against an empire, the Athenians sent troops. They tore down the Naxians' defensive walls and seized their small fleet of ships. Another member of the Delian League suffered a similar fate four years later when Cimon laid siege to Thasos.

The transformation of the Delian League into an Athenian empire persisted under the leadership of Pericles and his supporters. "The process" of Athens enforcing its will on others "was continued in the cases of other allies," Thucydides wrote, "as various circumstances

ALLIES FORCED TO OBEY ATHENS

Under both Cimon and Pericles, Athens increasingly treated its allies in the Delian League in a strict manner. Eventually, these allies were forced to swear the following oath to the Athenians:

> I will not revolt from the people of Athens by any manner of means, in word or in deed, nor will I obey anyone else who is in rebellion; and if anyone rebels I will denounce him to the Athenians; and I will pay the tribute which I persuade the Athenians to assess, and I will be an ally to the Athenian people as best as I can and as justly as I can, and will help and defend the people of Athens, if someone harms [them], and I will obey the people of Athens.[7]

arose." In most cases, Thucydides said, Athens claimed that some member states did not contribute to the Delian League the money or ships they had originally pledged:

> The Athenians insisted on obligations being exactly met, and made themselves unpopular by bringing the severest pressure to bear on allies who were not used to making sacrifices and did not want to make them. . . . [Thus, the Athenians forced] back into the alliance any state that wanted to leave it.[8]

Another move that made Athens unpopular with its allies involved the funds the Delian League's member states contributed to its upkeep each year. The monies were originally stored in a treasury on the island of Delos. In a bold move, Pericles eventually transferred the funds to Athens, saying they would be safer there. This provoked outrage far and wide, including among some Athenians. Also controversial was the fact that some of the money was being used to erect public buildings in Athens. Pericles' political enemies complained that Athens had lowered its reputation because many other Greeks viewed the transfer of the money from Delos as outright theft. It was especially bad, his opponents said, that Athens was using the funds that belonged to the Delian League to beautify Athens. Pericles firmly disagreed with these accusations. He said that the Athenians were not legally bound to tell their allies how their money was used as long as Athens continued to organize and lead the ongoing military actions against Persia.

BUSY ON MANY FRONTS

Relations with Delian League allies constituted only a small part of the vigorous foreign policy carried out by Pericles throughout his tenure as Athens's leading general. Under him and his supporters, the Athenians became involved in many overseas ventures and conflicts. Critics at home complained that the city was overextending itself and wasting valuable resources. But Pericles and his party controlled the Assembly. And that body consistently seemed pleased with the steady expansion of Athenian power and prestige.

One of the first such foreign adventures during Pericles' early years in power was an expedition to Egypt. At the time, the Persians occupied and controlled that ancient land. In 460 B.C., about a year after Ephialtes' murder, the Athenian government received a message from Inaros, king of Libya, a kingdom located west of Egypt. Inaros had just helped the Egyptians stage a rebellion against their Persian overlords. To hold the country, however, he needed outside aid. And as Thucydides told it:

> He called in the Athenians to help him. The Athenians happened to be engaged in a campaign against [the Persians in] Cyprus with 200 ships. . . . They abandoned this campaign, came to Egypt, and sailed from the sea up the Nile. They gained control of the river and two-thirds of [the Egyptian capital of] Memphis.[9]

While this contingent of Athenian troops was tied up in Egypt, Pericles and the other generals did not hesitate to commit more troops elsewhere. One of these

Athenians feast and play music at a banquet during the time of Pericles.

new ventures provoked Sparta because it involved two members of the Peloponnesian League. Made up of Sparta's allies, this organization was the Spartan counterpart of Athens's Delian League. One of the two states in question was Megara, located directly west of Athens. The other was Corinth, situated at the northeast corner of the Peloponnesus, the large peninsula making up the southern third of the Greek mainland. (Sparta itself was located in the southern sector of the Peloponnesus.)

Athens initiated trouble with these states in 459 B.C. by seizing Naupactus, an important port city located a few miles west of Corinth. This allowed the Athenians to interfere with Corinthian shipping for their own financial gain. The angry Corinthians, who had long been trade rivals of the Athenians, declared war. Almost immediately, Megara, which had recently been feuding with Corinth, decided to quit the Peloponnesian League and become Athens's ally. Not surprisingly, both of these developments irritated and worried Sparta.

THE WAR WITH CORINTH AND AEGINA

As the war began, Athens quickly took the initiative by building a defensive wall across the frontier lying between Corinth and Megara. This barrier prevented Sparta, Corinth, and other Peloponnesian states from moving troops and trade goods northward into mainland Greece. So the Spartans viewed erecting the wall as an act of war. For the time being, however, they seemed content to sit back and let the Corinthians do the fighting.

A few skirmishes occurred between small groups of Corinthian and Athenian ships. Then Corinth acquired a new ally of its own—the small island of Aegina—located in the Saronic Gulf a few miles from Athens's port town of Piraeus. Like Corinth, Aegina was a strong maritime power in the region. Also like the Corinthians, the Aeginetans had long resented Athenian interference in their shipping routes. And they hoped that their teaming up with Corinth would create an alliance strong enough to defeat what they saw as the arrogant and overbearing Athens.

Both Aegina and Corinth had made a serious mistake in opposing Periclean Athens, however. First, by this time Athens, long the most populous city-state in

Greece, was a military powerhouse, especially in naval affairs. Also, many Athenians felt that Aegina was a dangerous pest that lay too close to Athens for comfort. Pericles himself became famous for the colorful and cryptic remark that Aegina was an "eyesore of the Piraeus,"[10] one that badly needed removing. In 458 B.C. therefore, Pericles and his fellow generals coordinated an attack on Aegina. The Aeginetans' fleet was severely mauled in a sea battle in the Saronic Gulf. Then Athenian troops swarmed ashore on Aegina itself. They laid siege to its main town, which soon surrendered.

Meanwhile, Corinth fared no better against the energetic Athenians. One of Pericles' colleagues, Myronides, led an Athenian land army against a Corinthian force that was trying to invade Megara. At first, both sides claimed victory. But it rapidly became clear that the Athenians had bested their foe. The Corinthians eventually decided to withdraw but then met with an even worse disaster. "As the defeated Corinthians were retreating," Thucydides wrote,

> quite a large section of their army, coming under severe pressure [from the pursuing Athenians] and being uncertain of its route, plunged into an enclosure on someone's estate, which had a deep ditch all around it so that there was no way out. Seeing what had happened, the Athenians closed up the main entrance with their soldiers, and, surrounding the rest of the enclosure with light-armed troops, stoned to death all who were inside. This was a very severe blow to the Corinthians.[11]

⚔ THE LONG WALLS

Many Athenians heartily congratulated Pericles for humbling their trade rival, Aegina. He and the other Athenian strategoi also received high marks for their seemingly easy defeat of Corinth. In addition, word arrived that Athens's Egyptian expedition was still going well. Emboldened by their successes on many fronts, the Athenians now apparently felt confident enough make another move that was sure to anger Sparta. They knew that provoking the Spartans was always a calculated risk. After all, Sparta's phalanx (a battlefield formation consisting of several lines of soldiers standing one behind the other) was the most feared in Greece. Seeing the dreaded red cloaks of the Spartan troops approaching, some Greek troops were so afraid they simply turned and ran away.

Athens's leaders were willing to take this risk, partly because they believed they had a good way of defending against a Spartan attack. In the same year in which the Athenians besieged and defeated Aegina (458 B.C.), Pericles made a daring proposal to the Assembly. He pointed out that the defensive walls presently in place around Athens were not nearly formidable enough to repel a Spartan invasion. Even if the enemy could not get into the urban center, they could surround it and starve the inhabitants into surrendering. The remedy, Pericles insisted, was to erect high walls stretching all the way from the urban center to Piraeus, more than four miles distant. These Long Walls, as they came to be called, would create a secure lifeline to the sea. The Spartans would be unable to breach such walls, he said, so the Athenians would be safe behind them. And even if the Spartans destroyed Athens's fields and crops, the people could still get the food they needed by importing it through their fortified port of Piraeus.

SHOWDOWN AT TANAGRA

Predictably, the Spartans saw the creation of the Long Walls as still another example of Athenian boldness and aggression. The combination of these walls with the ones built earlier between Megara and Corinth seemed to Sparta a threat to the balance of power in southern Greece. Spartan leaders decided that Athens must be taught a lesson in humility. The question they faced was how to carry out a successful attack on the enemy, who was now protected—either by walls or the sea—in the west, south, and east.

The single option left for Sparta was to assault Athens from its only unprotected flank—the north. In the summer of 457 B.C., a force of fifteen hundred Spartan troops, plus ten thousand Peloponnesian allies, crossed the Gulf of Corinth. After reaching its northern shore, they marched eastward into Boeotia (bee-OH-shya). Lying directly north of Attica, Boeotia was the territory dominated by the ancient and venerable city-state of Thebes. The Thebans had long disliked the Athenians, and the plan was for the Spartan and Theban forces to combine for a major attack on Athens.

However, through intelligence reports, Pericles and his fellow generals got wind of what was happening. And

GREEK PHALANXES AT WAR

Heavy infantrymen in ancient Greece were called *hoplites* (perhaps from the Greek word *hopla*, meaning "heavy equipment"). They wore chest protectors made of bronze or layers of linen and helmets and greaves (lower-leg protectors) of bronze. They carried a bronze shield, and, for weapons, a thrusting spear with an iron tip and a short iron-bladed slashing sword. The hoplites most often fought in a formation known as the phalanx. It consisted of a mass of troops standing in ranks (lines), one behind the other. The uplifted shields of the men in the front rank formed a formidable protective barrier that was hard to penetrate. When a phalanx marched forward, the only thing that could stop it was another phalanx of equal or greater strength. The sight and sounds of two phalanxes crashing together were often described as "terrifying" and "awe-inspiring."

befitting their nature, they acted quickly and decisively. They led an army northward and surprised the Peloponnesians at Tanagra (about twenty miles east of Thebes).

Pericles and his colleagues then encountered a sudden surprise of their own. Just as the battle was about to commence, a solitary man, decked out in full armor, appeared and tried to take a place in the Athenian ranks. It was Cimon. Though technically still in exile, Plutarch wrote, he was "determined to clear himself of his supposed pro-Spartan sympathies by his actions and by sharing the dangers of his fellow countrymen."[12]

Pericles was not about have his former political enemy share in the glory of this great showdown with the Spartans. According to Plutarch, Pericles and his friends drove "Cimon away from the ranks on the ground that he was still in exile," and therefore had no right to fight in the army. Though successful in eliminating Cimon, Pericles had focused attention on himself and his own patriotism. "For that reason," Plutarch added, "it is believed that Pericles fought in this battle with greater courage than ever before and surpassed everyone in exposing himself to danger."[13]

Pericles managed to get through the battle in one piece. But overall the Athenians suffered a narrow defeat. In the days and weeks that followed, they worried that the Spartans would press their advantage and launch a full-scale invasion of Attica. This did not happen, however. Perhaps because they felt they were unprepared for such a massive undertaking, the Spartans withdrew from Boeotia and went home. (The Spartans were well-known for their reluctance to commit large numbers of troops in long campaigns far from home.)

Many Athenians, Pericles likely included, viewed Sparta's withdrawal as a sort of backhanded Athenian victory. Once more they were emboldened to assert their authority beyond their own borders. To punish Thebes for conspiring with Sparta, only two months after the fight at Tanagra the Athenians crushed a Theban force at Oenophyta (in southern Boeotia).

Disaster in Egypt

During Pericles' early years as Athens's most influential leader, the city's fortunes in its many ventures had been mostly positive. It soon became clear, however, that the Athenians had, as some had worried they would, overextended themselves. In recent years, Athens's troops in Egypt had rather easily defeated the small Persian forces that had been occupying that country. But in 456 B.C. the Athenian expedition ran into trouble when the Persian king struck back with a large army. The invaders swept across Egypt. And in 454, they wiped out nearly every man in the Athenian garrison. Some forty ships and as many as eight thousand men were lost, and the recent solid chain of Athenian victories over the Persians was broken.

Out of necessity, therefore, Periclean Athens temporarily put its enormous foreign ambitions on the back burner. Pericles and his associates recognized that, for the moment, they could not afford to get involved in a fight with Sparta. So they offered peace. Fortunately, for all involved, Cimon was about to return from his ten-year exile. In 451 B.C., Pericles prevailed on his former enemy to negotiate a truce with the Spartans. In Plutarch's words:

> This only goes to show how far in those days the differences between party leaders were a matter of political opinion. Their private feelings . . . could easily be set aside in the public interest, while even ambition, the most powerful of human passions, was subordinated to the country's welfare.[14]

Thus, exactly ten years after working so hard to get rid of Cimon, Pericles found himself working at his side. This was a tribute to the patriotism of both men, as well as the unique democratic system that empowered them.

5

PROMOTING DEMOCRACY AND CULTURE

The truce with Sparta negotiated by Cimon in 451 B.C. held more or less firm until Pericles himself worked out a more permanent treaty in 446. The latter agreement came to be known as the Thirty Years Peace. In essence, Athens agreed to keep out of Sparta's affairs. And Sparta agreed not to interfere in Athens's management of the Delian League. Neither party expressed a desire to be friends with the other or to overlook prior disputes.

Rather, the treaty bluntly recognized the reality that Greece was now firmly divided into two opposing blocs—one controlled by Athens, the other by Sparta. Each member of a bloc was expected to remain in it. Changing sides would only upset the balance of power in Greece. And the treaty was all about maintaining a status quo in which one side warily respected the borders and assets of the other. It was an uneasy peace, therefore, because the act of breaking it clearly could plunge the Greek world into a major war. Nevertheless,

Pericles and the Spartan leaders with whom he negotiated were willing to give the new agreement a chance.

For the moment, the treaty put a sort of damper on Athenian attempts at expansion. And that allowed Pericles and other Athenian leaders a chance to concentrate much of their time and energy on affairs at home. This is an apt point in Pericles' story, therefore, to consider his domestic achievements. As important and far-reaching as his foreign policies, they included reforms that made Athens's democracy more open. Pericles also oversaw extensive building programs that made Athens the showcase of the Greek world. He seemed to sense that these efforts would impart a kind of immortality to his city, a reputation that would long outlive him and his peers. In a brilliant piece of foresight, he correctly predicted, "Future ages will wonder at us, as the present age wonders at us now."[1]

A True Believer in Democracy

Certainly, people in both Pericles' day and later eras observed Athenian democracy with great interest, if not amazement. Even before Ephialtes and Pericles reduced aristocratic influences on the democracy, Athenians had more say in governing themselves than any citizen group in history. After Ephialtes' death, Pericles continued to push for democratic reforms. It is significant that most of these changes made the government more open and transparent and gave more power to ordinary citizens. "Under Pericles' leadership," Donald Kagan points out, the Athenian Assembly passed a series of laws that went far toward establishing a constitution as thoroughly democratic as the world had ever seen. It gave direct and ultimate power to its citizens in the Assembly and the popular law courts, where they made all decisions by simple majority vote, and provided for the selection of most public offices by lot, for the direct election of a special few [notably the generals], and for short terms of office and close control over all public officials.[2]

These facts go against attempts by Pericles' contemporary opponents, as well as critics in later ages, to paint him as a power-hungry leader. It is true that in foreign affairs he advocated Athens's iron-fisted domination of Athens's allies. But on the domestic front, within his own country, he hated any form of tyrannical rule. A true tyrant would not have fought so hard to give the people the power to punish him and even remove him from office at their will.

There is only one credible explanation for Pericles' relentless push for democratic reforms throughout his career. Namely, he was one of history's few genuine examples of a champion of democracy. It appears that he truly believed in that system and trusted that talented men like himself would inevitably rise to positions of power within it.

An Array of Democratic Reforms

Pericles' steadfast commitment to pure, open democracy is illustrated by one of his first democratic reforms. In the early years of the democracy, property qualifications existed for the archons. In other words, only men with a substantial amount of money and property were allowed to be chosen as archons by the voters. This rule had been made partly to ensure that aristocrats occupied the major public offices.

In 458 B.C., however, just three years after Pericles came to power in Athens, he passed a bill that changed all this. First, property qualifications for the archonship were eliminated. Now, men belonging to the hoplite class—farmers who doubled as soldiers in times of emergency—could become archons. Ex-archons still had the privilege of joining the Areopagus, now mainly a court for murder cases. So average citizens rapidly came to outnumber aristocrats in that body.

A couple of years later, another bill mandated that the archons be chosen by lot. Random selection ensured a blind and therefore arguably fairer selection process for the archonship. No longer could a person eager to acquire power and carry out a personal agenda become archon simply by persuading family and friends to vote for him.

A more far-reaching Periclean democratic reform introduced payment for public service. Athens's democratic system required the participation of a large proportion of the local population. In addition to the archons and generals, five hundred men served on the Council each year. Even greater numbers served in the judicial system. To make it impractical, if not impossible, to bribe or intimidate a majority of the members of a jury, a typical Athenian jury consisted of hundreds of citizens. Up to six thousand men (as women were excluded from serving as jurors) served on one or more juries each year. Before the advent of Pericles' reforms, jurors and other public servants were not paid. Many poorer men had to pass up the chance to serve because they could not afford to take time away from their regular jobs.

Instituting pay for jurors in the early 450s B.C. was a bold step that allowed for greater direct participation in the government by ordinary citizens. And this proved only the first step in a series of similar reforms. As time went on, councilmen, archons, assemblymen, and even soldiers and sailors on active duty came to be paid. By the middle of the following century, as reported by Aristotle, more than twenty thousand Athenian men received payment for public service each year. This is a remarkable figure when one considers that Athens had no more than fifty or sixty thousand male citizens at the time. (A modern analogy would be 60 million or more Americans playing direct roles in government and getting paid for it!)

Pericles and the radical democrats advocated other aspects of open democracy as well. One was complete freedom of speech. Any citizen could denounce a leader, even a general, on a street corner, in the Assembly, or anywhere else. Comic playwrights often launched scathing attacks on government officials, knowing full well that those leaders would likely attend the plays containing said assaults.

Such open criticism of both individuals and policies came to be expected by leaders and voters alike. And men of stature, like Pericles, were willing to accept public rebukes as part of the job of serving the people. Moreover, Pericles advocated that public service was not only an honor, but also a duty; and participation in public debate was a sign of good citizenship. "Here," he said (according to Thucydides),

> each individual is interested not only in his own affairs but in the affairs of state as well: even those who are mostly occupied with their own business are extremely well informed on general politics—this is a peculiarity of ours: we do not say that a man who takes no interest in politics is a man who minds his own business; we say that he has no business here at all.[3]

OPPONENTS OF DEMOCRACY

Not all of Pericles' governmental reforms were as popular or successful as payment for public officials, however. A good example is the new citizenship law he instituted in 451 B.C., the year in which Cimon returned from exile. The new statute limited Athenian citizenship to people whose parents were both born in Athens. The motivation for this law is somewhat unclear. It may be that Pericles and his supporters wanted to place still more limits on the powers of the traditional aristocracy. It had long been a common custom among Athenian nobles to have their sons or daughters marry people from other Greek states. This could help the family overshadow its neighbors by giving it access to foreign economic and military support. Pericles' citizenship law made such alliances of the privileged illegal. But it had unintended negative consequences. For one thing, it reduced social interactions between Athens and neighboring city-states, which created bad feelings with the people of some of those states. The new law also fostered some social problems within Athens itself. Athenian-born men were legally bound to choose only women born in Athens as marriage partners. So a number of men began having affairs outside of their marriages with foreign-born women, a practice that caused a good deal of problems within families.

For these reasons, many Athenians who believed in democracy, including some non-aristocrats, disliked the citizenship law. Meanwhile, some entrenched aristocrats found fault with some of Pericles' more popular reforms. These well-to-do men did not have to work at normal jobs, so they had plenty of free time to serve the people. In their view, this voluntary, philanthropic approach was the ideal. In contrast, they held, paying citizens to perform public service, as instituted by Pericles, was unethical. It was nothing less than a blatant attempt by the government to buy votes and popular support.

In addition to these critics, a small but often vocal minority of Athenians, also mainly aristocrats, outright disapproved of democracy. In their view, it was a corrupt and dangerous system because it placed too much power in the hands of low-class, uneducated people. Such people were too easily guided by their passions, the argument went, and should not be trusted with the reins of government. These views were expressed in an anonymous document penned in the 440s B.C. The author has come to be called the Old Oligarch. Among the educated aristocrats, he said, there was little injustice

Upper-class Men Should Rule

The anonymous fifth-century B.C. Athenian whom modern scholars call the Old Oligarch distrusted democracy. He felt that government should be run by the better educated men in the upper classes, rather than "ignorant" men in the lower classes. His remarks on the subject have survived in a document called *The Constitution of the Athenians*.

> Everywhere on earth the best elements [of society] are opposed to democracy. For among the best people [i.e., the aristocrats] there is minimal wantonness and injustice but a maximum of scrupulous care for what is good, whereas among the [common] people there is a maximum of ignorance, disorder, and wickedness. For poverty draws them rather to disgraceful actions. And because of a lack of money, some men are uneducated and ignorant. . . . As things are, any wretch who wants to can stand up [in the Assembly] and obtain what is good for him and the likes of himself. . . . If it is good government you seek, you will first observe the cleverest men establishing the laws in their own interest.[4]

and much care for "what is good." In contrast, "among the people there is a maximum of ignorance, disorder, and wickedness."[5]

JUSTIFYING NEW CONSTRUCTION PROJECTS

Fortunately for Pericles, such critics remained in the minority during the decades he was Athens's most important politician. The result was that most of the bills and policies he brought to the Assembly passed. Of particular importance were his proposals to launch an ambitious series of construction projects to beautify Athens.

Among the reasons Pericles cited for these initiatives was pride in the city itself. "I declare that our city is an education to Greece," he exclaimed in one of most famous speeches.

> Athens, alone of the states we know . . . [possesses] a greatness that surpasses what was imagined of her. . . . Mighty indeed are the marks and monuments of our empire. . . . You should fix your eyes every day on the greatness of Athens as she really is, and should fall in love with her. When you realize her greatness, then reflect that what made her great was men with a spirit of adventure.[6]

Another motivation for large-scale construction projects, Pericles, said, was the virtual eradication of unemployment. Such projects would keep thousands of people busy for years. Furthermore, there was enough money to pay all of them decent wages because Athens has acquired great wealth. According to Plutarch:

> He was . . . anxious that the unskilled masses, who had no military training, should not be debarred from benefiting from the national income, and yet should not be paid for sitting about and doing nothing. So he boldly laid before the people proposals for immense public works and plans for buildings, which would involve many different arts and industries and require long periods to complete.[7]

"In this way," Pericles himself is reported to have said,

> all kinds of enterprises and demands will be created which will provide inspiration for every art, find employment for every hand, and transform the whole people into wage-earners, so that the city will decorate and maintain herself at the same time from her own resources.[8]

Also, Pericles said, using a portion of Athens's wealth to erect impressive public buildings would advertise Athenian imperial greatness to the whole world. Indeed, once completed, these works were, in his words, sure to bring the city "glory for all time."[9] In this regard, the Periclean building programs achieved spectacular success. Plutarch later summed it up well in the following words:

> There was one measure above all which at once gave the greatest pleasure to the Athenians, adorned their city and created amazement among the rest of mankind, and which is today the sole testimony that the tales of the

ancient power and glory of Greece are no mere fables. By this I mean his construction of temples and public buildings.[10]

AN IMMENSE UNDERTAKING

In these building programs, new structures rose all across the Athenian territory of Attica. The main and by far most expensive focus of construction, however, was a new temple complex atop the Acropolis. Imposing temples and other public buildings had crowned the Acropolis before. But the Persians had destroyed these structures when they had swarmed into the deserted city in 480 B.C. Following the defeat of the invaders, the Athenians at first vowed not to rebuild. The ruins atop

The ruins of the Acropolis make for a very distinctive skyline.

the hill were to stand as a memorial to the victory and to those who had lost their lives fighting the barbarians. But by the 440s, a full generation had passed. And it was not difficult for Pericles to convince his fellow citizens that it was time to restore the Acropolis to its former glory.

In fact, the ambitious plan eventually aimed at far surpassing the size and splendor of the earlier structures on the hill. Aiding Pericles in drafting the plan was a group of brilliant artisans, including the architects Ictinus and Callicrates and the master sculptor Phidias. They envisioned a massive, ornately decorated entrance gate—the Propylaea, rising on the western flank of the Acropolis. After ascending a grand staircase and passing through this gate, visitors would reach the summit of the hill. Here, the main complex of temples, armories, statues, marble walkways, and altars would lie before them. The two principal temples in the complex—the Erechtheum and Parthenon—would be dedicated to Athens's patron, Athena. A huge altar to the goddess would rise in the space between these two great structures. And giant statues of her would be erected both inside and outside the temples.

Pericles and his talented associates realized that translating this elaborate and challenging plan into realty would be an immense undertaking. In addition to being enormously expensive, it would require a virtual army of artisans and laborers. Some would come from other Greek cities. But the bulk of these workers would be Athenians. It is a testament to Pericles' popularity and organizational abilities that he was able to marshal thousands of local people. Beginning in 447 B.C., freemen, slaves, citizens, and metics all gladly worked side by side in a concerted effort. Plutarch left behind a valuable description of the kinds of materials and workers involved:

> The materials to be used were stone, bronze, ivory, gold, ebony, and cypress-wood, while the arts or trades which wrought or fashioned them were those of carpenter, modeler, coppersmith, stone-mason, dyer, worker in gold and ivory, painter, embroiderer, and engraver, and besides these the carriers and suppliers of the materials, such as merchants, sailors, and pilots for the sea-borne traffic, and wagon-makers, trainers of draft-animals, and drivers for everything that came by land. There were also rope-makers, weavers, leatherworkers, road-builders, and miners. Each individual craft, like a general with an army under his separate command, had its own corps of unskilled laborers at its disposal. . . [and consequently] the city's prosperity was extended far and wide and shared among every age and condition in Athens.[11]

THE PARTHENON

The entire complex took decades to complete. But the largest single element—the Parthenon—was finished by 432 B.C. (The temple's main structural elements were in place by 438; the last six years were devoted to installing statues and sculptures and painting the building in bright colors.) The completed Parthenon was a marvel to behold. It was 237 feet long, 110 feet wide, and 65 feet high. More than twenty-two thousand tons of polished

Pericles made possible the construction of the Parthenon, which still stands today.

marble (quarried at nearby Mt. Pentelikon) went into its construction.

Eight giant columns graced the building's front porch, which faced west, toward the Propylaea. Atop these pillars rested a massive triangular space, or pediment, in which stood an array of statues sculpted by Phidias. The sculptures illustrated the central myth of the city's founding—a contest between Athena and the god Poseidon for possession of Attica and Athens. The eastern pediment, at the pinnacle of the Parthenon's back porch, had statues acting out Athena's legendary birth. (Supposedly she burst forth, clad in full armor, from the head of her divine father, Zeus.)

The inside of the Parthenon was no less spectacular than the outside. The main chamber, or cella, was 108 feet long, 62 feet wide, and 43 feet high. Dominating this space was Phidias's statue of Athena—a magnificent creation almost forty feet high and decorated with ivory and sheets of pure gold. The statue, known as the Athena Parthenos, was described a few centuries later by a Greek traveler, Pausanias, in his *Guide to Greece*:

> In the temple which they call the Parthenon . . . the cult image itself is made of ivory and gold. In the middle of her helmet there is placed an image of a sphinx [a mythical creature with the body of an animal and the face of a women] . . . and on each side of the helmet griffins are represented. . . . griffins are beasts which look like lions but have the wings and beak of an eagle. . . . The statue of Athena stands upright and wears a tunic that reaches to the feet, and on her breast [on a breastplate known as the aegis] the head of Medusa [a mythical

An Ancient Greek Describes the Erechtheum

Situated near the Parthenon, the Erechtheum temple was also dedicated to the goddess Athena. The second-century A.D. Greek traveler Pausanias provided the following description of the interior of the Erechtheum in his famous guidebook to Greek sites and monuments.

As you go in [to the temple], there are altars of [the sea god] Poseidon . . . and Hephaestos [god of the forge]. . . . The holiest of all the images [inside the temple] . . . is Athena's statue [the olive-wood Athena Polias]. . . . Rumor says it fell from heaven. Whether this is true or not, I shall not argue about it. [The sculptor] Callimachos made a golden lamp for the goddess. They fill this lamp with oil, and then wait [before refilling it] for the same day of the following year, and all that time the oil is enough to feed the lamp, though it shines perpetually night and day. . . . Over the lamp a bronze palm tree climbs to the roof and draws up the smoke.[12]

monster], made of ivory, is represented. In one hand she [Athena] holds a figure of [the goddess] Victory about four cubits [six feet] high and in the other she holds a spear; at her feet is placed a shield, and near the shield is a serpent. This serpent would be Erichthonios [a mythical attendant to Athena].[13]

An Everlasting Memorial

The completed Parthenon—along with the rest of the complex when it was finished—certainly accomplished two of its intended goals. One was to inspire awe in all those who gazed on it. The other was to trumpet the greatness of Athens to people in all places and ages.

Yet in pushing for the creation of the new Acropolis complex, Pericles had done much more. He had also tapped into and exploited to the utmost the creative energies of the Athenian people. In a way, he had allowed, indeed encouraged, a vigorous people in a pivotal moment in time to express itself in ways that no other group in history ever had. And the result was an everlasting memorial to his talent and vision as a leader and the innate talents of his people. As scholar John Miliadis, a noted expert on the Acropolis, so beautifully phrases it:

> It was not merely the passion for building [that motivated the achievement and made it great]. . . . It was not [just] the political consideration that the construction of these great works would give work to the people for many years . . . nor was it merely an exhibition of power. It was something deeper than all this. It was the irrepressible need of [a brilliant leader] and a whole

generation which took the highest intellectual view of life, to find a creative self-expression. This [leader and this] generation had dared to envisage man as raised to a godlike level. . . . The daring scheme was that of Pericles, the first of all the countless people who have been in love with Athens.[14]

6

TROUBLES WITH FAMILY AND FRIENDS

Much has been written about Pericles' political and military exploits. Often glossed over or ignored altogether are various aspects of his private life, including his relationships with family and friends. No comprehensive, detailed ancient narrative has survived about these relationships. However, Plutarch's biography of Pericles contains some illuminating information about Pericles' friends and controversial mistress, Aspasia. Other ancient writers briefly mentioned Pericles' sons and his foster son, the notorious Alcibiades. Prominent among these writers are the Athenian philosopher Plato and Athenian historian Xenophon (ZEN-uh-phon), both of whom flourished in fourth century B.C.

These and other ancient sources reveal that Pericles enjoyed much less success in his private affairs than he did in his public life. For one thing, it appears that he was not much of a family man or homebody, at least by ancient Athenian standards. Most Athenian men owned land and ran their estates, whether big or small, themselves. In contrast, Pericles spent very little time on his estate. He entrusted its maintenance to a steward named Evangelus, who managed it very efficiently.

Meanwhile, Pericles spent most of his time in Athens's urban center dealing with affairs of state. In fact, his almost constant preoccupation with politics seems to have taken its toll on other aspects of his private life. He went through a divorce and did not get along well with his sons. Also, his high public profile left him open to political attacks over his choice of friends and female companionship. During these attacks, the truth was likely often distorted. And as Plutarch commented, this often made it difficult for later historians to piece together what really happened:

> Writers who live after the events they describe find that their view of them is obscured by the lapse of time, while those that investigate the deeds and lives of their contemporaries are equally apt to corrupt and distort the truth, in some cases because of envy or private hatred, in others through the desire to flatter or show favor.[1]

An Unsatisfying Marriage

Certainly one area of Pericles' private life that later historians had trouble reconstructing was his marriage.

The exact date of the union is unknown, although various indirect pieces of evidence suggest it occurred about 463 B.C. This was shortly after his first election to the board of generals and shortly before Cimon's ostracism and Ephialtes' assassination. The name of Pericles' bride has also been lost, as have the details of the marriage.

However, certain facts about Pericles' relationship with his wife can be safely assumed from the nature of the marriage customs of the day. If the date of 463 B.C. for the wedding is correct, he was then about thirty-one or thirty-two. This is perfectly in keeping with custom; most Athenian men got married when they were in their late twenties or early thirties. Also following custom, his bride would have been about fourteen, fifteen, or sixteen, and therefore quite immature. In his Oeconomicus (or Estate Manager), Xenophon has an estate owner say:

> [My wife] wasn't yet fifteen years old when she came to me, and in her life up to then considerable care had been taken that she should see and hear and discover as little as possible. Don't you think that one should be content if all she knew when she came [to my house] was how [to turn wool into a cloak?] . . . I was content.[2]

If Pericles' marriage began this way, which is likely, it was not an alliance of equals, as is the ideal today. Again following custom, his young wife was confined to the home most of the time. There, with the aid of servants, she looked after the household, made clothes, cooked, and perhaps paid the bills. She would not have been allowed to go out in public by herself. Either Pericles, a male relative, or a male servant had to accompany her, and on such occasions she likely wore a veil over part of her face. (These precautions were intended to keep respectable women from interacting with strange men—that is, men who were not members of the immediate family or clan.)

Such lopsided relationships apparently satisfied most Athenian men. However, Pericles was not satisfied, as evidenced by his divorce in about the year 455 B.C. The exact reason for the split is unknown. But it is not unreasonable to assume that a man of his intelligence, educational level, and political interests may have been bored by a young woman with little or no knowledge of life or politics.

The divorce does not seem to have been unpleasant or mean-spirited, however. If an Athenian man wanted to divorce his wife, all he needed to do was order her to leave the house. And she simply passed from his authority back to her father's. In contrast, a woman who desired a divorce had to get an archon to give his permission. However the divorce was handled, it seems to have been an amicable one, as shown by what Pericles did later. Evidence shows that he willingly exerted the time and effort to arrange his ex-wife's marriage to a well-to-do Athenian named Hipponicus. However, some scholars dispute this.

THE SONS OF GOOD FATHERS

It appears that Pericles fared no better as a father than he did as a husband. He had two sons by his wife—Xanthippus and Paralus—both born by 460 B.C. Some interesting remarks about these young men appear in some of Plato's dialogues. In *Alcibiades* (which some scholars think Plato did not actually write), the title character says that Pericles' sons were simpletons. This rather harsh and unkind judgment is tempered somewhat in the dialogue *Protagoras*. Here, in a discussion about whether virtue can be taught, the title character asks, "Why, then, do the sons of good fathers often turn out ill?" He then gives some examples of illustrious Athenians whose sons were widely acknowledged to be "nothing in comparison with their fathers."[3] Among them are Paralus and Xanthippus.

General remarks like these are all that is known about Paralus. But Plutarch provided some more specific and quite revealing information about Xanthippus. The eldest of Pericles' sons, Xanthippus was "a spendthrift by nature," who "resented his father's passion for economy and the meager allowance he was given." In retaliation, when he was old enough, the young man engineered a shady deal behind his father's back:

> He approached one of Pericles' friends and borrowed money from him, pretending that this was on Pericles' instructions. When the friend later asked for repayment, Pericles, so far from settling the debt, brought a [legal] action against him. Young Xanthippus was furious and began openly to abuse [insult and denounce] his father, telling stories to raise a laugh against him [behind his back].[4]

This dysfunctional relationship between father and son is perhaps not surprising. Pericles was almost never home and probably spent little or no quality time with Xanthippus. Also, the boy likely saw both his father and his steward, Evangelus, as penny-pinchers who deprived him and his brother of the luxuries enjoyed by the sons of other prominent Athenians. At the same time, Xanthippus's personal traits and failings must be taken into account. He appears to have lacked his father's talents, self-discipline, and keen sense of community responsibility.

PERICLES AND ALCIBIADES

Pericles' parenting woes were not confined to his biological children. In 447 B.C. (or perhaps the following year), one of his closest friends, a man named Cleinias, died. Most often in such situations, any children involved passed to the custody of the father's closest male relative. But apparently Cleinias had, while he was still living, made other arrangements. He made it clear that if he should die, he wanted Pericles to raise his two sons.

The boys—Alcibiades and Cleinias—were about five and two respectively when Pericles took them in. Not much is known about young Cleinias. At one point, Pericles asked his own brother, Ariphron, to take charge of the boy, but only six months later Ariphron sent Cleinias back. It is possible that the boy exhibited severe emotional and/or behavioral problems.

Much more is known about Alcibiades, who later became one of Athens's most colorful and infamous

ALCIBIADES' PERSONAL GIFTS

Pericles' foster son, Alcibiades, was a larger-than-life individual who played a key role in Athenian affairs in the last years of the fifth century B.C. Though ultimately a rogue and troublemaker, Alcibiades was known for his physical and mental gifts. This description comes from Plutarch's biography of this controversial figure.

> As for his physical beauty, we need say no more than that it flowered at each season of his growth in turn, and lent him an extraordinary grace and charm, alike as a boy, a youth, and a man. [The great Athenian playwright] Euripides' saying that even the autumn of beauty possesses a loveliness of its own is not universally true. But if it applies to few others, it was certainly true of Alcibiades on account of his natural gifts and his physical perfection. Even his lisp is said to have suited his voice well and to have made his talk persuasive and full of charm.[5]

characters. According to Plutarch, who penned a biography of him, "he was a man of many strong passions, but none of them was stronger than the desire to challenge others and gain the upper hand over his rivals."[6] Even as a child, Alcibiades was self-centered, headstrong, undisciplined, and devious. He also became extremely ambitious and early set his sights on entering politics. Plutarch suggests that this goal was partly inspired by the larger-than-life public image of the young man's illustrious foster father. Also, Alcibiades surrounded himself with people who admired his audacious personality and wanted to see him acquire positions of power and influence:

> His tempters played upon . . . his love of distinction and his desire for fame, and in this way they pressed him into embarking on ambitious projects before he was ready for them. They assured him that once he entered public life he would not merely eclipse the other generals and politicians, but even surpass the power and prestige which Pericles had enjoyed.[7]

It is unclear what Pericles thought about Alcibiades' political ambitions. In fact, very little is known about the personal relationship between these two huge historical personalities. Certainly it is at least noteworthy that a man with Pericles' reputation for honesty and democratic principles raised a boy who grew up to be an unscrupulous man with little or no respect for the law.

Some light may be shed on the situation by a tract from Xenophon's *Memorabilia*. In it, Pericles and a teenaged Alcibiades discuss the law as it might be meted out by a democratic assembly. And the youth reveals his disdain for the ability of the common people to place restrictions on the well-to-do. Although based on hearsay, and perhaps fabricated, the exchange does seem to present the real positions of both men. "I hear people being praised for being law-abiding," Alcibiades supposedly told Pericles,

> "and I presume that nobody can rightly win this praise if he does not know what law is." "Well," said Pericles, "it's not at all a difficult object you're seeking, Alcibiades, if you want to find out what law is. When the people, meeting together, approve and enact a proposal stating what should or should not be done, that is a law.". . . [Alcibiades asked] "If the minority enacts something not by persuading the majority but by dominating it, should we call this violence or [law]?" "It seems to me," said Pericles, "that if one party, instead of persuading another, compels him to do something . . . this is always violence rather than law." [Alcibiades asked] "Then if the people as a whole uses not persuasion but its superior power to enact measures against the propertied classes, will that be violence rather than law?"[8]

It is probably safe to say that Pericles spent as little quality time with Alcibiades as he did with Xanthippus and Paralus. So it is not surprising that Alcibiades grew up to be very different than Pericles.

THE UNCONVENTIONAL ASPASIA

In contrast, Pericles eventually found ample time for another relationship with a woman. In the early 440s B.C., about six or seven years following his divorce, he asked a *hetaira* named Aspasia to live with him. In ancient Athens, *hetairai* (translated literally as "companions") were consorts. Most were foreigners in the sense that they came from other Greek cities. And unlike most Athenian women, hetairai were highly educated. Plato's contemporary, the Athenian orator Demosthenes, famously remarked that men in his city had wives to look after the house and the hetairai for companionship.

Aspasia, who hailed from Miletus, became more than simply a fond companion to Pericles, however. It appears that the two genuinely and deeply loved each other. This was unusual in a society in which most close male-female relationships consisted of arranged marriages. According to Plutarch, Pericles was drawn to Aspasia primarily because of her unusual political wisdom and felt real passion, what today would be called romantic love, for her. After Pericles divorced his wife, Plutarch said, he and Aspasia lived together. And "every day, when he went out to the marketplace and returned, he greeted her with a kiss."[9]

Many people today would find this a charming and romantic situation. But in fifth-century B.C. Athens it was scandalous. Society had no qualms about men associating with hetairai on a temporary basis. But actually living with a hetaira as if she was a wife was completely unacceptable. Making matters worse, the couple had a child together, who was both illegitimate and, thanks to Pericles own citizenship law, a noncitizen (because Aspasia was not a native Athenian). As a result, Pericles paid a heavy public and political price for the right to some private and personal happiness. "Unconventional relationships always attract public attention," University of Louisville scholar Robert B. Kebric points out,

> but when they involve such high-profile personalities as Aspasia and Pericles, who also had political enemies with whom to contend, we should expect a large body of negative comment. The comic poets were particularly unkind, identifying Aspasia with women in mythology who had made heroes . . . look ridiculous or caused their death.[10]

Such insults eventually escalated into a more serious and dangerous attack on Aspasia. In 438 B.C., a man named Hermippus brought her to court on charges of

THE SON OF PERICLES AND ASPASIA

The son born to Pericles and Aspasia was also named Pericles. Because of the citizenship law the elder Pericles had earlier sponsored, the boy was born a noncitizen, without full civic rights. In this way, Pericles became a victim of his own legislation. Later, after the death of his two biological sons, he pleaded with the members of the Assembly to suspend the law in his case. According to Plutarch, "he asked this so that the name and lineage of his house should not die out for want of an heir." The Assembly granted this request, and the younger Pericles became a full citizen. Years later, following his father's death, he was elected general and served his country in the Peloponnesian War.

impiety, lack of belief in or respect for the gods. She was also accused of convincing free-born Athenian women to become consorts for Pericles. (Many Athenians also blamed her for the Athenian attack on Samos, saying that she convinced Pericles to side with her native city of Miletus against the Samians.) Pericles himself defended her in the trial. He made a personal plea to the jurors, insisting that the charges were without foundation; and according to one ancient source, he got so emotional that at one point tears streamed down his face. Aspasia was acquitted, although verbal attacks on her continued.

PERICLES' FRIENDS IN JEOPARDY

Aspasia was not the only close associate of Pericles who came under public attack. Hoping to hurt him politically and maybe even bring him down, his opponents prepared to put his old teacher, Anaxagoras, on trial. As in Aspasia's case, the charge was lack of belief in the gods, an accusation easy to make and sure to inflame public passions. Someone proposed that a law be passed, Plutarch recalled, with wording "to the effect that anybody who did not believe in the gods or taught theories about celestial phenomena should be liable to prosecution, and this was aimed to cast suspicion on Pericles through Anaxagoras."[11] While this measure was before the Assembly, Pericles naturally became very worried for his old friend's safety. So he smuggled Anaxagoras out of the city and thereby allowed the old man to avoid the stress and embarrassment of a trial.

However, another close associate of Pericles—the great sculptor Phidias—was not so fortunate. In the same year that Aspasia and Anaxagoras were attacked (438 B.C.), Phidias faced false charges, too. The sculptor was first accused of stealing some of the gold he had been allotted to use in decorating the Athena Parthenos, the great statue of the goddess that stood inside the Parthenon.

To Phidias's and Pericles' relief, Plutarch wrote, "the charge of embezzlement was not proved."[12] This was because of Pericles' own foresight. When the statue was under construction, he had Phidias make the sheets of gold easily removable. That way, if at some future date the city was in dire need of cash, the gold could be collected, melted down, and used to help the people. With Phidias now in jeopardy, Pericles challenged the prosecutors to take down the gold sheets and weigh them. They did so, and sure enough, all the gold was accounted for. So they had to drop the theft charge against Phidias.

Almost immediately, though, Pericles' opponents leveled a second charge against the aging sculptor—impiety. The specific accusation involved Phidias's images carved on the huge shield resting alongside the Athena Parthenos. The sculpted scene showed several ancient Athenian heroes fighting the Amazons. (This legendary tribe of warrior women had supposedly threatened Athens in the dim past.) According to the prosecutors, one of the human figures in the scene closely resembled Phidias himself; and another seemed to represent Pericles. As Kagan points out:

This is a third-century Roman replica of the shield of the statue of Athena that once stood in the Parthenon. On it, Pericles can be seen in the center with his foot on top of a defeated Amazon.

This is the sort of amusement engaged in by many artists in the Italian Renaissance, but it was a daring and dangerous joke to play in the fifth century B.C. No living human being had ever been shown on a Greek temple before. . . . To carve recognizable people on the statue of the goddess was far too bold for the ordinary citizen. . . . Most Athenians remained religious in the traditional way. . . . Religious fears and superstitions always laid close to the surface, and the attack on Phidias brought them into the open.[13]

Unlike the first charge against the sculptor, therefore, the second one stuck. The jury found him guilty. Plutarch claimed that Phidias was thrown into a

THE IMPIETY CHARGE AGAINST PHIDIAS

Enemies of Pericles claimed that Phidias had insulted and disrespected the gods by including images of himself and Pericles in a sculpted scene on the shield held by a giant statue of Athena. This charge was politically motivated, frivolous, and mean-spirited, to be sure. Yet it appears that Phidias did purposely carve himself and Pericles onto the goddess's shield. A few centuries later, Plutarch studied the sculpture (which was later lost, along with the statue itself) up close and wrote:

Phidias (on stairs) shows off his statue of Athena. In the center, Pericles and Aspasia marvel at the sculptor's work.

> He carved a figure representing himself as a bald old man lifting up a stone with both hands, and . . . he introduced a particularly fine likeness of Pericles fighting an Amazon. The position of the hand, which holds a spear in front of Pericles' face, seems to have been ingeniously contrived to conceal the resemblance, but it can still be seen quite plainly from either side.[14]

jail cell and soon died there. However, most modern scholars think that Plutarch's information in this instance was inaccurate and that the sculptor was exiled.

 ## A New Breed of Enemy

Phidias's conviction and all the negative publicity surrounding the trials caused Pericles much personal anguish and regret. Pericles' political opponents ultimately failed to topple him from his powerful position, however. To his credit, he managed to retain the trust and backing of most Athenians during this difficult period in his life and career.

Pericles must have begun to worry about his future, however. In addition to their mean-spirited nature, there had been something ominous about these recent attacks. Namely, the men who had launched them were not the usual sort of enemies Pericles was used to fighting. For more than two decades he had been opposed by what might be called the right-wingers of Athens. They were almost always well-to-do, conservative aristocrats who distrusted democracy and thought they knew what was best for the people. They also tended to be pro-Spartan.

The men who had attacked Aspasia, Anaxagoras, and Phidias, however, were not a part of the old guard. Among a new and potentially more dangerous breed of enemies, they were in a sense left-wingers. They were commoners who had managed to acquire money and social position through success in the trades and commerce. Many lacked solid educations and distrusted intellectuals like Anaxagoras and Aspasia. (They also saw Aspasia as an uppity woman who did not know her place and, therefore, was a threat to the established system of male dominance.) In the realm of foreign affairs, these men supported Athens's policy of expansion and autocratic treatment of its Delian League allies. They disliked the Spartans and seemed more willing than Pericles was to risk provoking them. However, the main goal of Pericles' new opponents was domestic in nature. Namely, they wanted to get rid of him and other staunch democrats and place themselves in positions of power.

Ironically, Pericles' new enemies were partly the product of the democratic revolution he had helped to expand. Athens's democratic system had placed a lot of power in the hands of the common people. And now some of them were learning to abuse that power to achieve their own ends, just as the aristocrats had in the past. This created a new political reality for Pericles. From now on, he would need to watch out for attacks from all sides of the political spectrum.

7

ON THE ROAD TO TOTAL WAR

Interest in the high-profile trials that took place in Athens in 438 B.C. was not confined to that city. Developments in Athenian politics often affected the Greek world as a whole, just as political developments in the United States frequently affect the rest of the modern world. So the leaders of other Greek city-states eagerly awaited runners bearing periodic news reports about the trials. Few Greeks cared whether Aspasia and Phidias were convicted or acquitted. Mostly, people wanted to see how the negative publicity would affect Pericles. After all, as everyone knew, he was the real target of the Athenian prosecutors. If his opponents managed to topple him from power, the face of Athenian politics was sure to change, and that would inevitably affect all of Athens's neighbors.

Of these neighbors, perhaps none followed the trials more closely than Sparta. Though most Spartan leaders

A CRITIC OF PERICLES

The ancient sources say that Pericles was very proud of himself in the wake of his final victory over the Samian rebels. Many prominent Athenians stepped forward to congratulate him after he delivered a moving funeral speech over the Athenians who had died in the campaign. However, some Athenians recognized the darker, more ominous aspects of the Samian affair. One woman expressed these reservations particularly well. Elpinice, sister of Pericles' former political rival, Cimon, confronted Athens's leading general and told him in a sarcastic tone:

> This was a noble action, Pericles, and you deserve all the garlands for it. You have thrown away the lives of these brave citizens of ours, not in a war against the Persians . . . such as my brother Cimon fought, but in destroying a Greek city which is one of our allies.[1]

Pericles listened to these stinging words quietly and then, without answering them, walked away.

did not like Pericles, they had a vested interest in him and the success or failure of his policies. Eight years before (446 B.C.), they had signed the Thirty Years Peace with him. Athens and Sparta had vowed to stay out of each other's affairs, and so far both sides had honored the agreement. True, the Samian crisis of 440–439 B.C. had made Sparta and its allies uneasy. Led by Pericles, Athenian troops had intervened in a dispute between Samos and Miletus. Athens had defeated Samos, ended its dispute with Miletus, and forced the Samians to adopt democracy.

As the Spartans viewed it, these events were still another example of Athenian aggression. However, they did not directly threaten the Thirty Years Peace. Samos and Miletus were members of the Delian League and therefore part of Athens's own sphere of influence. As long as the Athenians did not intrude into the affairs of Sparta and the Peloponnesian League, the Spartans were not legally bound to act.

Perhaps Spartan leaders breathed a sigh of relief when Pericles emerged from the trials with his authority intact. They likely saw him, at least for the moment, as the lesser of two evils. After all, those who sought to bring him down were even more anti-Spartan than he was. Still, in the eyes of most Spartans, Pericles was a dangerous man who needed to be watched closely. Indeed, his potential as a troublemaker seemed to be confirmed in the years immediately following the trials. Periclean Athens did begin to intrude into the affairs of Sparta's allies. And the result was a series of crises that gripped the Greek world.

During these tense times, several Greek states begged Sparta to intervene, to attack Athens and whittle it down to size. The reserved Spartans, who were reluctant to go to war, repeatedly chose to refrain from violence. But how long could they be expected to show restraint? That was a question that many Greeks, including a growing number of Athenians, increasingly asked as the Greek states drew closer and closer to the brink of total war.

Aspasia, a consort, was Pericles's main female companion after his divorce.

THE CRISIS IN EPIDAMNUS

Actually, Pericles and the Athenians did not instigate the first of the crises that pushed Sparta and its allies toward war. Only later did Athens get involved in and thereby escalate a series of warlike incidents centered on the island of Corcyra, situated off Greece's northwestern coast. Corcyra had been colonized a few centuries before by Corinth, now a Spartan ally and enemy of Athens. That made Corinth in a sense the mother city of Corcyra. However, mother and child had been at odds for several generations. They had fought frequently over shipping rights and control of various colonies.

One of these colonies was the city-state of Epidamnus, located on the mainland coast about one hundred twenty miles north of Corcyra. Epidamnus had been colonized by Corcyreans, so its mother city was Corcyra, while Corinth was its grandmother city. In 435 B.C., the aristocrats in Epidamnus, who had long been in control, were overthrown by the local democrats.

In an effort to regain power, the ousted aristocrats soon joined forces with foreign pirates and began attacking the city.

Desperate, the Epidamnian democrats appealed to their mother city, Corcyra, for aid. But the Corcyreans refused to get involved. As Thucydides told it, that prompted the Epidamnians to seek help from their grandmother city, a move that ended up widening the conflict:

> When the people in Epidamnus realized that no help was forthcoming from Corcyra, they . . . begged the Corinthians to come to their help and not allow them to be destroyed. The Corinthians agreed to come to their assistance. They felt they had a good right to do so, since they regarded the colony as belonging just as much to them as to Corcyra; and at the same time, they hated the Corcyreans because they failed to show to Corinth the respect due from a colony to the mother city. . . . The Corinthians . . . sent out a force consisting of [soldiers and settlers]. . . . When the Corcyreans discovered that the settlers and the troops had arrived at Epidamnus, they reacted violently. . . . They put to sea with twenty-five ships, which were soon followed by another fleet.[2]

The Corcyreans demanded that the Epidamnian democrats give up power and reinstate the aristocrats. The Epidamnians promptly refused the ultimatum. And just as promptly, the Corcyreans began laying siege to the city.

Back in Athens, Pericles and his fellow democrats watched these events with keen interest. As champions of democracy, they were naturally tempted to send aid to the besieged Epidamnian democrats. But Pericles was likely wary of getting involved because of Corinth's role in the dispute. Corinth was a Spartan ally. And if hostilities erupted between Athens and Corinth, Sparta might see it as a breach of the Thirty Years Peace.

For the moment, therefore, Pericles and his associates refrained from entering the fray. They watched as Corcyra and Corinth continued to anger and provoke each other. In the process, the dispute between local Epidamnian aristocrats and democrats faded into the background; and the larger differences between Corcyra and Corinth came to the fore.

Corcyra Against Corinth

Eventually, the Corinthians declared war and sent a fleet of seventy-five warships north toward Epidamnus. The Corcyreans intercepted them with eighty ships of their own and a major battle ensued. Thucydides reported that the Corcyreans were victorious after destroying fifteen Corinthian ships. Then, following up on their win, the Corcyreans attacked Leucas, a Corinthian colony, and pillaged its lands.

Although these reverses had badly damaged the Corinthians' prestige, in their view they had not lost the war. In the two years that followed, they built huge new war fleets and manned them with sailors from across the Greek world. Seeing this ominous military buildup, the Corcyreans became alarmed. They had no allies, since

GREEK TRIREMES

The trireme was the most common type of Greek warship in the era in which Pericles lived. The average Athenian trireme was roughly 130 feet long and 18 feet wide. It had three banks of oars, 62 in the upper bank and 54 each in the middle and lower banks, for a total of

 170. Most of the rowers were professionals who came from the city's lower classes. A few were hired from other Greek cities. In addition to the 170

rowers, a trireme's crew included 15 sailors (or deck hands), a flute player who kept time for the rowers, ten (or occasionally more) hoplites (armored fighters), and four archers. Triremes had sails as well as oars. But the sails were generally used only in open seas. When close to coastlines, and also during battle, the sails were lowered and the vessels maneuvered solely by oar power.

they belonged to neither the Delian League nor the Peloponnesian League.

Perhaps not surprisingly, therefore, the Corcyreans turned to the only Greek state that had naval forces large enough to stand up to the new Corinthian fleets—Athens. In 433 B.C., Corcyra sent ambassadors to Athens. They hoped to convince Pericles and the Athenian Assembly to form an alliance with Corcyra. Now it was Corinth's turn to be alarmed.

"When the news of this move reached Corinth," Thucydides wrote, "the Corinthians also sent representatives to Athens, fearing that the combined strength of the navies of Athens and Corcyra would prevent them from having their own way in the war with Corcyra."[3]

Members of both foreign delegations spoke before Athens's Assembly. Pericles, the other generals, and the Athenian citizenry listened intently as the Corcyreans made their case. First, they said, if Athens became Corcyra's ally, it would "not be helping aggressors, but people who are the victims of aggressors." Also, the world would admire the Athenians for their generosity. The Corcyreans also argued: "It is not a breach of your treaty with Sparta if you receive us into your alliance. We are neutrals."[4] Finally, they suggested that a major war with Sparta and its allies was inevitable. Would it not make sense for the Athenians to prepare for that conflict by strengthening their sea power through an alliance with Corcyra?

Then it was the Corinthians' turn to speak. They argued that it would be wrong for the Athenians to form an alliance with Corcyra. Because Corinth was a Spartan ally, they said, the treaty Athens had made with Sparta applied to Corinth, too. The ambassadors explained that Corcyra was Corinth's enemy. Therefore, Corinth would view an Athenian alliance with Corcyra as an act of war against Corinth. That would be a clear breach of the Thirty Years Peace. "The right course, surely," the Corinthians said,

> is either for you to preserve strict neutrality or else to join us against them. . . . You should be conscious that we are in one of those critical situations where real friendship is to be gained from helping us and real hostility from opposing us. . . . Thus, you will be acting as you ought to act and at the same time you will be making the wisest decision in your own interests.[5]

BATTLE AT THE SYBOTA ISLANDS

After the Corinthian and Corcyrean ambassadors had spoken, Pericles addressed the assembly. According to Plutarch, he "persuaded the Athenians to send help to Corcyra." Clearly, Pericles and the generals wanted "to bring over to their side an island with a powerful navy at a time when the Peloponnesians" posed an imminent threat to Athens. However, it appears that Pericles also desired to be cautious and if possible to avoid open warfare with Corinth. After the Assembly voted to go forward with the alliance with Corcyra, "Pericles sent a squadron of no more than ten ships" to Corcyra.[6] This small force was intended more for defensive purposes than offensive ones and hopefully would not provoke war. Donald Kagan explains:

> Pericles' decision was an effort at what is called in current jargon "minimal deterrence." There need be no war, the Athenians indicated by their action, if Corinth would refrain from attacking Corcyra and seizing her fleet. The presence of an Athenian force was proof that Athens was determined to prevent a shift in the balance of naval power. But its small size showed that the Athenians would not seize the opportunity to diminish or destroy Corinthian power. If the ploy worked, the Corinthians would sail home without a fight and the crisis would pass. . . . Even if the Corinthians chose to fight, Pericles seems to have hoped that the Athenian fleet could stay out of the battle.[7]

But this risky ploy did not work. Not only did the Corinthians choose to fight, the Athenians were not able to avoid getting involved. Corinth sent an enormous fleet of 150 warships. Near the Sybota Islands, just south of Corcyra, these vessels encountered an opposing armada of 110 Corcyrean ships, supplemented by the ten Athenian triremes Pericles had sent. At first, the commanders from Athens kept their triremes out of the battle. Thucydides said that they were afraid of violating the orders they had been given—to fight only if Corcyra itself came under attack. Soon, however, the Athenians saw that the Corcyreans were in trouble and felt obliged to help them. The Athenian ships entered the fray and soon they and the Corinthian vessels were engaged in a death struggle.

For a while, it looked as though the Corinthians might win the battle. They managed to drive much of the enemy force back to the Corcyrean beaches. But then the entire situation rapidly changed. About twenty more Athenian ships suddenly appeared on the horizon. (Against Pericles' advice, the Assembly had sent them to back up the original ten.) Fearing that even more Athenian triremes were about to arrive, the Corinthians began to retreat. The next day, envoys from the Athenian and Corinthian sides met. "Peloponnesians," the Athenian envoy said,

> we are not starting a war and we are not breaking the treaty. These Corcyreans are our allies, and we came here to help them. We shall do nothing to stop you if you wish to sail in any other direction. But if you sail against Corcyra or against any part of her territory, then we shall do our best to prevent you.[8]

PLEAS FOR SPARTA TO ACT

This attempt to placate the Corinthians was in vain, however, for the damage had been done. For the time being, the Corinthians withdrew from Corcyrean waters. But they strongly felt that the Athenians, whom they had long distrusted, had pushed them too far. As Thucydides put it, the incident at the Sybota Islands "gave Corinth her first cause for war against Athens."[9]

This did not mean that Corinth was prepared to go to war against Periclean Athens alone. The Corinthians realized that they had no chance against the combined

107

More Like a Land Battle

In his Peloponnesian War (Rex Warner's translation), Thucydides described the opening moments of the battle of the Sybota Islands, in which fleets of Corinthian, Corcyrean, and Athenian warships were involved.

> The fighting was of a somewhat old-fashioned kind, since they were still backward in naval matters, both sides having numbers of hoplites [armored infantrymen] aboard their ships, together with archers and javelin throwers. But the fighting was hard enough, in spite of the lack of skill shown: indeed, it was more like a battle on land than a naval engagement. When the ships came into collision, it was difficult for them to break away clear, because of the number [of ships] engaged and of their close formation. In fact, both sides relied more for victory on their hoplites, who were on the decks and who fought a regular pitched battle there while the ships remained motionless. . . . Everywhere in the battle confusion reigned, and there was shouting on all sides.[10]

might of Athens and its Delian League allies, plus its newest ally, Corcyra. Corinth clearly needed Sparta and its own formidable allies to intervene. So the Corinthians complained loudly to the Spartans, saying that in siding with Corcyra, Athens had broken the Thirty Years Peace.

The notoriously slow-to-act Spartans reacted by holding a conference in their own city. They invited any Peloponnesians, or any other Greeks for that matter, who had grievances against the Athenians, to come and speak. Not surprisingly, the speech given by the Corinthian ambassadors was the most emotional and angry. They boldly told the Spartans that their continued peaceful posture toward Athens was naïve and only encouraged Athenian aggression:

> Many times before now we told you what we were likely to suffer from Athens, and on each occasion, instead of taking to heart what we were telling you, you chose instead . . . to consider that we were speaking only about our own grievances. The result has been that you did not call together this meeting of our allies before the damage was done. . . . You can see yourselves how Athens has deprived some states of their freedom and is scheming to do the same for others . . . and that she herself has for a long time been preparing for the eventuality of war. . . . And it is you [i.e., the Spartans] who are responsible for all this. It was you who in the first place allowed the Athenians to fortify their city and build the Long Walls after the Persian War.[11]

To bolster their case that the Spartans had waited too long to act, the Corinthians launched into a comparison of Athenian boldness and Spartan reluctance. No specific mention was made of Pericles. But everyone involved knew that Pericles and his radical democratic faction had shaped the policies that had led Athens to this critical juncture in Greek affairs. The Athenians were always innovators, the Corinthian ambassadors said. In contrast, the Spartans rarely originated ideas or actions. Athenians never hesitated, while Spartans hung back. "While you stay at home," the Corinthians told the Spartans, the Athenians are "always abroad." Also, "if they aim at something and do not get it, they think they have been deprived of what belonged to them already. . . . They are by nature incapable of either living a quiet life themselves or of allowing anyone else to do so."[12]

Finally, the Corinthians implored the Spartans to act. The Spartans' inactivity had to end, they said. They must quickly gather their renowned and feared army and invade the Athenian territory of Attica. "Do not force the rest of us in despair to join a different alliance," they said daringly, "If we do so, no one could rightly blame us. . . . If you will only make up your minds to act, we will stand by you. . . . Think carefully over your decision. From your fathers was handed down the leadership of the Peloponnesus. Maintain its greatness."[13]

THE MEGARIAN CRISIS

Pericles and his fellow generals received a full account of what was said in the conference in Sparta. (This was because a group of Athenians had been visiting that city on unrelated business at the time. They were allowed to attend the meeting of the gathered delegates.) To his relief, no doubt, Pericles learned that the Corcyrean crisis had not caused Sparta to act. Despite the forceful plea made by the Corinthians, the Spartans still refused to declare war.

One of the Spartan kings (two of which ruled jointly), Archidamus, stated Sparta's position. First, he said, the war the Corinthians were proposing was likely to be large scale and destructive. Second, the Spartans would have to fight not only Athens, but also its allies. And some of these were located far from Sparta and had a great deal of experience in naval affairs (whereas the Spartans had no significant naval tradition). Third, Athens and several of its allies were wealthy and populous, both major advantages in prosecuting a war. "How, then, can we irresponsibly start a war with such people?" Archidamus asked the Corinthians. "What have we to rely on if we rush into it unprepared?" True, he conceded, the Spartans' heavy infantry was superior to that of Athens or any other Greek state. Yet Athens controlled considerable territories outside of the Attic peninsula and could import all the supplies it needed through its fortified port. "If we can neither defeat them at sea nor take away from them the resources on which their navy depends," Archidamus said,

> we shall do ourselves more harm than good. . . . What I do suggest is that we should not take up arms at the present moment. Instead, we should . . . put our grievances before them. . . . As for being slow and cautious—which is the usual criticism made against us—

111

there is nothing to be ashamed of in that. . . . "Slow" and "cautious" can equally well be "wise" and "sensible."[14]

If in the months that followed Pericles and other influential Athenian leaders had shown the same restraint Archidamus had, war might have been averted. But they did not. Not long after the Sybota Islands battle (perhaps early in 432 B.C.), Pericles pushed through a trade embargo against Athens's neighbor, Megara. The Megarians were forbidden from conducting commerce at any Delian League port; and Athenian ships kept foreign merchant vessels from landing at Megara.

Some critics—both in ancient and modern times—have accused Pericles of imposing the embargo to force the Peloponnesians into a major war. But this is highly unlikely. The embargo was probably another calculated risk intended to assert Athens's authority while stopping short of all-out war. The Megarians, who by now had rejoined the Peloponnesian alliance, had recently declared their solidarity with the Corinthians. Pericles likely felt that Athens had to do something to discourage Corinth's allies from joining its warlike cause. The action against Megara, therefore, may have been designed to send a warning. Namely, the Athenians did not want war but would impose economic sanctions on any state that seemed to be siding with Corinth against Athens.

THE SPARTANS FINALLY ACT

The problem was that the embargo, the second of Pericles' daring calculated risks in less than a year, backfired. As the months rolled by, the Megarians held firm and refused to ask Athens for quarter. So the blockade continued and the Megarians began to starve. Meanwhile, despite pleas from around the Greek world for him to drop the embargo, Pericles remained just as firm in his own position. "It seems likely that the Athenians might have avoided war," Plutarch wrote,

> if only they could have been persuaded to lift their embargo against the Megarians and come to terms with them. And since it was Pericles who opposed this solution more strongly than anyone else and urged the people to persist in their hostility towards the Megarians, it was he alone who was held responsible for the war.[15]

Certainly a majority of Spartan leaders saw Pericles and his aggressive stance as warlike. Archidamus, who knew Pericles personally and probably understood his true motives, continued to argue for negotiation rather than war. But the Spartan king was overruled by the city's elders and other leaders. (The Spartan kings held authority mainly in military and religious matters and had to follow the will of the elders in most other areas.) According to Thucydides, one of the elders said:

> "Spartans, those of you who think that the treaty has been broken and that the Athenians are aggressors, get up and stand on one side. Those who do not think so, stand on the other side," and he pointed out to them where they were to stand. They then rose to their feet and separated into two divisions. The great majority were of the opinion that the treaty had been broken.[16]

It was agreed to give Pericles and his countrymen one last chance for peace—a demand for Athens to abandon the Megarian embargo and its other aggressive policies. Few in Sparta thought this would be successful, however. Slowly but methodically, the long-reluctant Spartans now began preparing their truly formidable army for all-out war.

8

WAR POLICY AND DEMISE

The Spartan decision to give Athens one last chance to avert war may well have been influenced by King Archidamus. He did not want to see his country become mired down in a long, bloody conflict. Also, unlike most Spartans, he believed that Pericles did not want war either. So Sparta sent envoys to Athens to demand one last time that Athens stop the embargo of Megara. The Athenians refused. Soon afterward, three Spartan ambassadors arrived in Athens to deliver a final ultimatum. According to Thucydides, they said: "Sparta wants peace. Peace is still possible if you will give the Greeks their freedom."[1]

The Athenian Assembly met to consider the Spartan ultimatum. As had been the case for the past three decades, the most eagerly anticipated and powerful speaker was Pericles. Also, as in the past, he was not ready to give in to Spartan demands. In fact, a major theme of his impassioned speech was that the Spartans rarely, if ever, actually negotiated; rather, they made demands, which they backed up with the threat of unleashing their fearsome army. This was not acceptable, Pericles said (as reported by Thucydides):

> It is laid down in the treaty that differences should be settled by arbitration. . . . The Spartans have never once asked for arbitration, nor have they accepted our offers to submit to it. They prefer to settle their complaints by war . . . and now they come here . . . trying to give us orders.

Pericles went on to warn that going to war with the Spartans and their allies would be dangerous and risky. Yet that should not deter a people as proud and resilient as the Athenians:

> We must realize that this war is being forced upon us, and the more readily we accept the challenge, the less eager to attack us will our opponents be. We must realize, too, that . . . from the greatest dangers, the greatest glory is to be won. . . . We must live up to the standard [our forefathers] set. We must resist our enemies in any and every way and try to leave to those who come after us an Athens that is as great as ever.[2]

The Athenians once more followed the advice of their favorite leader. And thus it came to pass that in 431 B.C. the two opposing blocs into which the Greek world had long been divided at last came to death grips. Thucydides later summarized the great scope of the coming conflict: "The two sides were at the very height of their power. . . . I saw, too, that the rest of the Greek world was committed to one side or the other. . . . This was the greatest disturbance in the history of the Greeks, affecting also a large part of the non-Greek world."[3]

It is impossible to know what Pericles was thinking as his country entered the most devastating war Greece had ever known. Apparently he was confident that Athens would, as it had so often in the past, meet the challenge and ultimately prevail. At that moment he could not foresee what would turn out to be a much darker future. Athens would not prevail. And its greatest leader would not live long enough to witness the shame and anguish of defeat and surrender.

THE OPPOSING STRATEGIES

In retrospect, however, it is easy to see why Pericles was so confident that Athens would be victorious. First, it had many allies, most of whom were located outside of mainland Greece. They included most of the Ionian cities and Aegean islands, along with Corcyra. Athens and these allies virtually controlled the seas, which meant that the Athenians would have access to seemingly unlimited resources and supplies.

In contrast, Sparta's main allies were largely confined to the southern Greek mainland. They included Corinth and most of the other Peloponnesian cities, Megara, and Thebes and its tiny neighbors in Boeotia. Granted, Corinth was a great sea power. But its fleets could be effectively neutralized by those of Athens and its allies. Pericles likely reasoned, therefore, that Sparta and its own allies would be forced to make do with the

GREECE DURING THE PELOPONNESIAN WAR

MACEDONIA
Stagira
Byzantium
Abydos
PERSIAN EMPIRE
THESSALY
Ambracia
Aegean Sea
Sardis
Thebes
EUBOEA
Athens
ACHAEA
Corinth
Ephesus
Ionian Sea
Argos
SPARTA
Sparta

Athens and other Athenian Allies	The Spartan Confederacy	Neutral Greek States

Though Athens had the stronger navy, the Spartans quickly marched their hoplites into Athenian territory.

resources they could gather from the mainland. And in the long run they would drain these resources.

The fact that the Athenian alliance was mostly a sea power and the Spartan alliance mainly a land power also dictated the basic military strategies of the combatants. Pericles fully anticipated that the Spartans would invade Attica in full force. The Spartan hoplites would mow down any defenders who got in their way. The invaders would also burn Athenian farms and crops and spread fear and confusion far and wide. That way, the Spartans hoped, the Athenian people would see the error of their ways, surrender quickly, and allow the Spartans to avoid a prolonged conflict, a concept they abhorred.

In response to this enemy strategy, Pericles planned a novel counterplan, one that no other Greek state had ever adopted on a large scale. When the invasion began, the Athenians would not even attempt to engage the lethal Spartan hoplites. Instead, the natives would retreat behind the Long Walls. There, they would be safe. In the meantime, Athenian and allied ships, still in control of the seas, would keep them well supplied. Eventually, according to the plan, the Peloponnesians would tire of their assaults and end them.

ATTACKS ON ATTICA AND PERICLES

Sure enough, just as Pericles had anticipated, the Spartans launched their land invasion. In May 431 B.C., an army of at least thirty-five thousand troops entered Attica from the west. About three to four thousand of these were heavily armored Spartan soldiers. Perhaps another eleven thousand were Boeotians, and the rest were from Sparta's Peloponnesian allies. As the Athenians withdrew behind their walls, as planned, the invaders found that they had no one to fight. So they proceeded to devastate the countryside. They burned houses and barns, cut down olive trees, and confiscated or destroyed crops.

From their vantage behind the Long Walls, the Athenians watched this pillage and destruction of their homeland. And their horror and frustration rapidly grew to a fever pitch. As Thucydides told it, many were no longer so confident in Pericles' plan and called on him to abandon it:

> Their land was being laid waste in front of their very eyes—a thing that young men had never seen happen and that old men had seen only at the time of the Persian invasion. Naturally enough, therefore, they felt outraged by this, and wanted, especially the young, to march out and stop it. There were constant discussions, with violent feelings on both sides. . . . [Many] were furious with Pericles and . . . abused [denounced] him for being a general and not leading them out to battle, and put on him the whole responsibility for what they were suffering.[4]

But Pericles remained resolute. Though he, too, was frustrated by the ongoing destruction, he was certain that his plan would work in the long run. According to Plutarch, he attempted to pacify those who were itching to fight by pointing out "that trees, even if they are lopped or cut down, can quickly grow again, but that you cannot easily replace the men who fall in battle."[5] Thus, he decided not to call for a meeting of the Assembly, worried that its members might force him to abandon his controversial plan. Instead, he closed the city's gates, placed guards along the walls, and ignored the many complaints he received from his fellow citizens. Meanwhile, Pericles' political enemies threatened to destroy him, a number of his friends begged him to change his mind, and the comic playwrights lampooned and derided him and his policies.

THE ATHENIANS STRIKE BACK

Pericles soon showed that he possessed potent ammunition to counter both his Athenian critics and the Peloponnesian invaders. At home he could, at least for the moment, trust in a strong power base he had built up over the years. It consisted of various "soldiers, administrators, and politicians" Donald Kagan points out, who

> shared political opinions and served as generals along with him, while accepting his informal leadership. The support of such men made it possible for Pericles to withstand the storm of criticism he encountered and to restrain the many Athenians who urged him to attack the Peloponnesian army.[6]

But though Pericles did not send the Athenian infantry to face the deadly Spartan hoplites, he did order his countrymen to go on the offensive in other ways. In particular, he tried to exploit the significant advantages of the sea power Athens possessed. While the Spartans and their allies were running amok in Attica's countryside, the Athenians launched a large naval force. It consisted of some one hundred Athenian warships, fifty Corcyrean vessels, and several others supplied by Delian League allies. A number of the ships carried hoplites and archers. The strategy of this armada was to counterattack the enemy in his own homeland. The allied ships ravaged the Peloponnesian coasts and sacked or destroyed a number of coastal towns and farms.

The Athenians also landed on the island of Aegina (which Pericles had earlier called the "eyesore of the Piraeus"), a Spartan ally. As a naval power in its own right, Aegina had the potential to interfere with ships entering and leaving Athens's port. So Pericles ordered his troops to remove the island's entire population and to replace it with Athenians. That way, the waters near the strategically important Piraeus would remain secure.

Finally, Pericles took advantage of the fact that the Peloponnesians at first did not occupy Attica on a permanent basis. In the fall, they withdrew and returned to their own homes and farms. They planned to renew their invasion in the following spring. But in the meantime the Athenians enjoyed a welcome respite, emerged from behind their walls, and did their best to repair the damage the enemy had inflicted.

At the same time, Pericles himself led an army of at least fourteen thousand troops into neighboring Megara. "This was certainly the biggest Athenian army that had ever taken the field," Thucydides said.[7] These soldiers laid waste to Megarian farms and villages, much as Megara's allies had recently done in Attica. The war was clearly becoming a contest to see which side could inflict, as well as sustain, more destruction and suffering than the other.

Pericles' Great Funeral Oration

During the winter of 431/430 B.C., a temporary lull in the fighting allowed both sides to tally their losses and bury their dead. At this early juncture in the conflict, not many Athenian soldiers had died yet. But those who had lost their lives were widely viewed as heroes. Thucydides provided the following vivid account of how Athens honored its war dead:

> Two days before the ceremony the bones of the fallen are brought and put in a tent which has been erected, and people make whatever offerings they wish to their own dead. Then there is a funeral procession in which coffins of cypress wood are carried on wagons. . . . One empty bier is decorated and carried. . . . This is for the missing, whose bodies could not be recovered. Everyone who wishes to . . . can join in the procession. . . . The bones are laid in the public burial place, which is in the most beautiful quarter outside the city walls. . . . When the bones have been laid in the earth, a man chosen by the city for his . . . general reputation makes an appropriate speech in praise of the dead.[8]

No other Athenian had as large a reputation as Pericles. So it is not surprising that the citizens chose him to deliver the oration at the funeral of the war's first casualties. His speech, viewed later as one of the greatest in history, consisted of much more than the usual mourning of and praise for the dead. Pericles wisely took the opportunity to speak directly to the Athenian people about the war. In general, he sought to justify Athens's participation in the conflict and to remind his countrymen what they were fighting for. In so doing, he painted a masterful verbal picture of Athenian democracy and cultural superiority:

> Our system of government does not copy the institutions of our neighbors. It is more the case of our being a model to others. . . . Our constitution is called a democracy because power is in the hands not of a minority, but of the whole people. . . . Everyone is equal before the law. . . . No one, so long as he has it in him to be of service to the state, is kept in political obscurity because of poverty. . . . We are free and tolerant in our private lives; but in public affairs we keep to the law. . . . Our love of what is beautiful does not lead to extravagance; our love of things of the mind does not make us soft. We regard wealth as something to be properly used, rather than as something to boast about. . . . Taking everything together, then, I declare that our city is an education to Greece. . . . Our adventurous spirit has forced an entry into every sea and into every land; and everywhere we have left behind us everlasting memorials of good done to our friends.[9]

Long after other existing cities and peoples had been forgotten, Pericles went on to say, Athens would be remembered for its greatness. In a way, therefore, Pericles said, those who had died, and would later die, for Athens would achieve a sort of immortality. Such men "knew their duty." They gave Athens their lives,

> to her and all of us, and for their own selves they won praises that never grow old. . . . Their glory remains eternal in men's minds, always there to stir others to speech or to action. . . . It is for you to try to be like them.

PERICLES PRAISES ATHENIAN COURAGE

During the course of the great funeral oration Pericles delivered in 430 B.C., he compared certain key Athenian political and military practices to those of the enemy—Sparta—as recounted in this excerpt from Thucydides' *Peloponnesian War* (Rex Warner's translation):

> Our city is open to the world, and we have no periodical deportations in order to prevent people [from] observing or finding out secrets which might be of military advantage to the enemy. This is because we rely, not on secret weapons, but on our own real courage and loyalty. There is a difference, too, in our educational systems. The Spartans, from their earliest boyhood, are submitted to the most laborious training in courage; we pass our lives without all these restrictions, and yet are just as ready to face the same dangers as they are. Here is a proof of this: When the Spartans invade our land, they do not come by themselves, but bring all their allies with them. Whereas we, when we launch an attack abroad, do the job by ourselves.[10]

Make up your minds that happiness depends on being free, and freedom depends on being courageous.[11]

THE PLAGUE

Many Athenians took heart at these words. They concluded that Pericles was right—that their city was special and worth fighting and sacrificing for. So they began preparing to carry on the war. In the spring of 430 B.C., as expected, the Peloponnesian forces returned and once more began pillaging Attica's countryside. As before, the Athenians retired behind the Long Walls and waited.

This time, however, the Spartan invaders were aided by an unexpected ally. In May of that year, a terrible plague struck Athens. Thucydides reported that rumors claimed it had originated in Ethiopia (in Africa) and spread from there to Egypt and eventually northward into the eastern Mediterranean region. The historian, then about thirty, contracted the disease himself. Fortunately he survived it and later described its debilitating symptoms:

> People in perfect health suddenly began to have burning feelings in the head. Their eyes became red and inflamed. Inside their mouths there was bleeding from the throat and tongue, and the breath became unnatural and unpleasant. . . . Before long, the pain settled on the chest and was accompanied by coughing. Next the stomach was affected, with stomach-aches and with vomiting. . . . The skin was rather reddish and livid, breaking out into small pustules [boils] and ulcers. . . . If

people survived this critical period, then the disease descended into the bowels, producing violent . . . and uncontrollable diarrhea, so that most of them died later as a result of the weakness caused by this. It affected the genitals, fingers, and toes, and many of those who recovered lost the use of these members. Some, too, went blind.[12]

Modern experts point out that these symptoms are somewhat similar to those of typhoid fever, pneumonic plague, and several other serious illnesses. However, the exact identity of the infectious killer that ravaged Periclean Athens remains unknown.

Whatever it was, the plague spread quickly through the crowded temporary settlements that had been erected behind the Long Walls. At least 20 percent of the city's population died. And many others were blinded, otherwise incapacitated, or orphaned. Public discontent was understandably high and many people vented their frustrations by blaming Pericles for the disaster. "They were urged on by his personal enemies," Plutarch wrote,

who convinced them that the plague was caused by the herding together of the country folk into the city. Here, in the summer months, many of them lived huddled in shacks and stifling tents. . . . The man responsible for all this, they said, was Pericles . . . [who they claimed had] left them penned up like cattle to infect each other.[13]

PERICLES' LAST WORDS

Faced with these accusations, Pericles called a meeting of the Assembly and gave a moving speech in his own

127

"THEY DIED LIKE FLIES"

In this section of his vivid description of the plague that struck Athens in the spring of 429 B.C., Thucydides stresses the factor of overcrowding, which, he says, contributed to the high death toll.

A factor which made matters much worse than they were already was the removal of people from the country into the city, and this particularly affected the incomers. There were no houses for them, and, living as they did during the hot season in badly ventilated huts, they died like flies. The bodies of the dying were heaped one on top of the other, and half-dead creatures could be seen staggering about in the streets or flocking around the fountains in their desire for water. The temples in which they took up their quarters were full of the dead bodies of people who had died inside them.[14]

defense. The distraught people rejected his words, however. They stripped him of his rank as general and levied a large fine on him.

This denunciation and demotion turned out to be temporary. It soon became clear to many Athenians that they had removed their best leader. According to Plutarch: "The people tried other generals and politicians . . . to carry on the war, but they found that none of these possessed a stature or an authority that was equal to the task of leadership. So the city came to long for Pericles and summoned him back to the Assembly."[15] Thus, in the spring of 429 B.C. the fickle Athenians set aside their recent grievances against Pericles and elected him strategos still again.

As it turned out, however, this time Pericles was unable to serve out his term. That summer he, like so many of his countrymen had, contracted the plague. The disease "gradually wasted his bodily strength and undermined his noble spirit," Plutarch said.[16] As he lay on his deathbed, Pericles' friends and fellow generals praised him for his military exploits and victories. But he took exception to this. Supposedly with his last breath, he told them that he was astonished

> that they should praise and remember him for exploits which owed at least as much to good fortune as to his own efforts, and which many other generals had performed quite as well as himself, while they said nothing of his greatest and most glorious title to fame. "I mean by this," he went on, "that no Athenian ever put on mourning because of me."[17]

Some Athenians had every right to dispute these last words of Pericles. After all, over the years numerous Athenian soldiers had died, causing their relatives to mourn, as a result of his policies. But few Athenians could deny that in many ways he had been a truly extraordinary leader, one that could not be easily replaced. Plutarch summed it up well:

> After his death, the course of events soon brought home Pericles' worth to the Athenians and made them sharply conscious of his loss. . . . [They were] compelled to admit that no man . . . was ever so moderate, or, when clemency was called for, better able to maintain his dignity. Henceforth, the public life of Athens was to be polluted by a rank growth of corruption and wrongdoing, which Pericles had always checked and kept out of sight, thereby preventing it from taking an irresistible hold. Then it was that that power of his, which had aroused such envy . . . stood revealed in its true character—as the saving bulwark of the [democratic] state.[18]

9

PERICLES' LEGACY

Whatever his fellow citizens thought about him when he was alive, after Pericles' death most Athenians sorely regretted his passing. As Athens recovered from the plague, the great war raged on. And the death toll on both sides steadily rose. Increasingly, it became clear to the Athenians that the leaders who succeeded Pericles lacked his vision, wisdom, honesty, and ability to unite the populace in concerted action. "Indeed," Thucydides wrote,

> during the whole period of peace-time when Pericles was at the head of affairs, the state was wisely led and firmly guarded, and it was under him that Athens was at her greatest. . . . And after his death, his foresight with regard to the war became even more evident. For Pericles had said that Athens would be victorious if she bided her time, and took care of her navy, if she avoided trying to add to the empire during the course of the war, and if she did nothing to risk the safety of the city itself. But his successors did the exact opposite.[1]

131

Men of Lesser Talents and Abilities

Of the first group of these successors, the most notable were a right-wing politician named Cleon and a wealthy citizen named Nicias. Nicias, who had served as a general alongside Pericles, advocated that the Athenians should swallow their pride and ask the Spartans to make peace. In contrast, Cleon insisted that Athens must continue fighting until the enemy was destroyed. An excerpt from Plutarch's *Life of Nicias* gives an idea of the mediocre leadership abilities of both men:

> Cleon commanded a large following because of his practice of "pampering the people and finding jobs for all," but even those whom he went out of his way to win over, when they saw the greed and effrontery of the man, turned to Nicias as their leader. Nicias, by contrast, wore an air of gravity . . . blended with earnestness and caution and this won him the confidence of the people by giving the impression that he was positively afraid of them. Although he was by nature timid and inclined to defeatism, his good fortune enabled him to conceal his lack of resolution.[2]

Neither of these men, nor any other Athenian leader, was able to get the Athenian people to adopt a firm and successful war or peace policy. So the conflict dragged on and on. Each year the Spartans and their allies invaded and ransacked Attica, while the Athenians hid behind their walls.

Then, in 422 B.C., Cleon died in battle. This allowed Nicias and the peace party to gain some ground.

The result was a treaty with the Spartans, which appropriately came to be known as the Peace of Nicias. For a while, it seemed as if the great war might be over.

But soon a new leader rose to prominence in Athens—Pericles' foster son, Alcibiades. More charismatic, talented, and daring than either Cleon or Nicias, Alcibiades was also more unprincipled and dangerous. He proved this by convincing three of Sparta's allies (Elis, Mantinea, and Argos) to quit the Peloponnesian League and join Athens. This time the Spartans were not reluctant or slow to act. They swiftly crushed the rebels, then turned their fury on the Athenians. The great war resumed with a vengeance.

As if he had not done enough damage, Alcibiades went on to cause Athens one of the worst setbacks in its long history. He got the Assembly to authorize an immense expedition, consisting of more than a hundred ships and tens of thousands of men. The goal was to attack and defeat the Greek city of Syracuse, on the island of Sicily (just south of Italy). Alcibiades argued that this would bring Athens huge stores of supplies, foodstuffs, and manpower. These would give the Athenians an edge over Sparta and make an Athenian victory certain. Incredibly, the Assembly agreed to the audacious and ill-conceived plan, putting Alcibiades and Nicias in joint command of the venture. In a nutshell, it turned out to be a spectacular failure. Alcibiades turned traitor and joined the Spartans; Nicias proved an incompetent military commander; and nearly all the men were lost.

Alcibiades led the Athenian military into a tremendous defeat at the Greek city of Syracuse.

Athens fought on, though it never fully recovered from the Sicilian disaster. Finally, in 404 B.C., after twenty-seven years of nearly relentless war, the Athenians surrendered. The Spartans forced them to tear down the Long Walls and give up most of their ships. The victors even helped a group of Athenian autocrats to institute a tyrannical government. (However, the freedom-loving Athenians threw out the despots and reinstated their democracy a few months later.)

 ## SYMBOLS OF A GLORIOUS PAST

Thus, largely as a result of the failings of its post-Periclean leaders, Athens lost the Peloponnesian War. So the immediate effect of Pericles' anti-Spartan policies was the city's decline and the abrupt end of its cultural golden age. Never again would the Athenians display the intensity of national energy, ambition, and cultural achievement that they had during the Fifty Years.

Nevertheless, the democratic principles Pericles had championed lived on. So did the Parthenon and other magnificent structures he had sponsored. These political and cultural attainments, along with Pericles himself, became symbols of a glorious past. In the fullness of time, not only the Athenians, but all Greeks came to see Pericles and his works as among the very best things their civilization had produced.

More centuries elapsed, and the rising power of Rome, master of the Italian peninsula, eclipsed that of the Greeks. By the end of the first century B.C., all of the Greek city-states and kingdoms had been absorbed into the Roman realm, now ruled by a dictator. Democracy as the Athenians of Pericles' time had known it was dead. Yet the monuments and arts of the Greeks and their proud history remained. More importantly, the Romans greatly admired Greek culture and absorbed a great deal of it, creating the cultural fusion that later ages came to call Greco-Roman, or classical.

A Man for the Ages

In the fifth and sixth centuries A.D., Rome, too, declined and went the inevitable way of all human civilizations. Yet various aspects of the Greco-Roman experience survived within the medieval European cultures that grew upon the wreckage of the Roman Empire. And the democratic and architectural legacy of Pericles and

The design of the columns of the Roman Temple of Saturn was influenced by Greek architecture.

Periclean Athens remained imbedded within this cultural legacy.

In early modern times, democracy at last began to reemerge in the world. Those who experimented with it looked to the past—especially the Greco-Roman past—for examples. The founding fathers of the infant United States viewed the democracy of Periclean Athens as too radical, just as Pericles' aristocratic opponents had long before. So early American leaders were more influenced by the ideals of republican Rome. In time, though, the openness of Periclean democracy came to be admired, not only in the United States but across the world. And in the West, Pericles became a champion of human freedom and a hero of those who struggled to achieve and defend it. In World War I, for instance, many London buses displayed posters bearing excerpts from his great funeral oration. (The English saw a parallel between Periclean Athens's struggle against autocratic Sparta and democratic Britain's fight against German tyranny.)

The modern Western world came to admire Pericles in other ways as well. Most historians, for example, view him as a national leader of extraordinary talent and insight who played a key role in the creation of Athens' cultural golden age. "Few eras in human history can compare with the greatness achieved by Athens under the leadership of Pericles in the fifth century B.C.," Donald Kagan writes,

> With a population of some two hundred fifity thousand, Periclean Athens produced works of literature, sculpture, and architecture that stand as models, inspirations, and wonders to this day. It witnessed the birth of historical writing, which one of its citizens [Thucydides] brought at once to an unsurpassed level of sophistication. It was the home of scientific speculation of an intensity and originality rarely, if ever, equaled.[3]

No less impressive was the legacy of Periclean art and architecture. In particular, the mammoth construction project he initiated atop the Acropolis has become nothing less than a wonder of the world. The Parthenon is often called the most perfect and beautiful structure ever erected. And even in an advanced state of ruin, it retains an air of splendor, grace, and nobility. Moreover, both ancient and modern observers agree that the

Parthenon, like other Periclean buildings, possesses a quality of timelessness. Among the ancient descriptions, none is more apt or moving than Plutarch's. "It is this above all," he wrote,

> which makes Pericles' works an object of wonder to us—the fact that they were created in so short a span, and yet for all time. Each one possessed a beauty which seemed venerable [impressive in old age] the moment it was born, and at the same time a youthful vigor which makes them appear to this day as if they were newly built. A bloom of eternal freshness hovers over these works of his and preserves them from the touch of time.[5]

John Miliadis provides an equally eloquent modern evaluation of the Periclean Acropolis, calling it a monument to what a free people might achieve when

These statues can be seen on the Erechtheium, a temple that is part of the Acropolis.

inspired by a great leader. "No other work of man has been so national in its roots, and so international in its fruits," he says. "None was more the product of its own age, and none has meant so much to all future ages. Nothing is less a relic of the past, and more perennially present."[6]

Miliadis's insightful vision of the Acropolis might well serve as a metaphor for Pericles and his own achievements. In spite of some personal shortcomings and mistakes, he was the foremost man of his time. And in many ways, he made possible one of humanity's greatest political and cultural expressions. Because the core elements of that expression—particularly democracy—have endured, and ultimately triumphed, he was also a man for the ages.

CHRONOLOGY

ca. 508 B.C.—An Athenian aristocrat named Cleisthenes and his supporters transform Athens's government into the world's first democracy.

ca. 500–323 B.C.—Greece's Classical Age, in which Greek arts, architecture, literature, and democratic reforms reach their height.

499 B.C.—The Greeks of Ionia (in western Asia Minor) rebel against the Persians, who had taken control of the region about four decades before.

ca. 495 B.C.—Pericles, who is destined to become the leading Greek statesman of the century, is born in Athens.

490 B.C.—Persia's King Darius I sends an expedition to sack Athens; the Athenians decisively defeat the invaders at Marathon, northeast of Athens.

484 B.C.—Pericles' father, Xanthippus, is ostracized (banished); Pericles follows his father into exile.

480 B.C.—Darius's son, King Xerxes, invades Greece at the head of a huge army; a Greek war fleet, led by the Athenian statesman Themistocles, defeats the Persian fleet at Salamis, southwest of Athens.

479 B.C.—The Greeks are victorious over the Persians at Plataea, north of Athens, and at Mycale, in Ionia.

ca. 479–429 B.C.—The period that later Greeks will come to call the Fifty Years, in which Athens reaches its political and cultural height.

478 B.C.—Athens helps to form the Delian League, an alliance of over a hundred city-states, with the goal of protecting Greece from further Persian attacks.

ca. 473 B.C.—Themistocles is ostracized.

472 B.C.—Pericles gains notoriety by sponsoring *The Persians*, a play by the Athenian playwright Aeschylus.

ca. 465 B.C.—Pericles is elected as one of Athens's ten generals for the first of many times.

461 B.C.—Pericles' chief political opponent, Cimon, is ostracized; Pericles' close associate, Ephialtes, is assassinated; Pericles, becomes Athens's most influential leader.

ca. 460–455 B.C.—Birth of the Athenian historian Thucydides, whose book about the Peloponnesian War is one of the two chief ancient sources about Pericles' career.

457 B.C.—Pericles finishes construction of the Long Walls, a fortified corridor leading from Athens's urban center to its port, Piraeus; the Athenians and Spartans meet in battle at Tanagra, near Thebes.

454 B.C.—An Athenian expedition sent earlier to liberate Egypt from Persian rule incurs severe losses; amid controversy, Pericles transfers the treasury of the Delian League from the island of Delos to Athens.

447 B.C.—Pericles organizes an enormous construction project aimed at erecting a major new temple complex atop Athens's Acropolis.

446 B.C.—Pericles engineers the Thirty Years Peace, a treaty between Athens and Sparta.

440–439 B.C.—The Athenians under Pericles lay siege to the island state of Samos and install democracy there.

438 B.C.—The Athenians dedicate the nearly finished Parthenon temple to the city's patron goddess, Athena.

435–433 B.C.—Athens is drawn into a conflict between the Greek states of Corcyra and Corinth.

432 B.C.—At Pericles' urgings, Athens imposes a trade embargo on the neighboring state of Megara.

431 B.C.—Sparta declares war on Athens, thereby starting the Peloponnesian War, which quickly draws in almost all of the Greek city-states.

429 B.C.—Pericles contracts a deadly plague, which has been ravaging Athens for months, and dies.

415 B.C.—Pericles' foster son, Alcibiades, convinces the Athenians to send a large military expedition to Sicily in hopes of conquering the Greek city of Syracuse; the expedition turns out to be a disaster for Athens.

404 B.C.—The Athenians surrender, ending the Peloponnesian War and Athens's cultural golden age.

ca. A.D. 45–50—Birth of the Greek biographer and moralist Plutarch, whose biography of Pericles is the other chief ancient source about Pericles.

CHAPTER NOTES

CHAPTER 1. BATTLING THE SAMIANS

1. Thucydides, *The Peloponnesian War*, trans. Rex Warner (New York: Penguin, 1972), p. 101.

2. Plutarch, *Life of Pericles*, in *Parallel Lives*, excerpted in *The Rise and Fall of Athens: Nine Greek Lives by Plutarch*, trans. Ian Scott-Kilvert (New York: Penguin, 1960), p. 192.

CHAPTER 2. BORN IN A PIVOTAL TIME

1. Plutarch, *Pericles*, in *Rise and Fall of Athens: Nine Greek Lives by Plutarch*, trans. Ian Scott-Kilvert (New York: Penguin, 1960), p. 167.

2. Herodotus, *The Histories*, trans. Aubrey de Sélincourt (New York: Penguin, 1972), p. 382.

3. Ibid., pp. 429–430.

4. Donald Kagan, *Pericles of Athens and the Birth of Democracy* (New York: Free Press, 1991), p. 17.

5. Ibid., p. 18.

6. Plato, *Protagoras*, in *Plato*, trans. Benjamin Jowett (Chicago: Encyclopedia Britannica, 1952), p. 46.

7. Kagan, pp. 20–21.

8. Plutarch, *Pericles*, p. 168.

9. Ibid., p. 169.

10. Ibid.

11. Anaxagoras, fragment, quoted in Philip Wheelwright, ed., *The Presocratics* (New York: Macmillan, 1966), p. 162.

12. Plutarch, *Pericles*, p. 169.

13. Ibid., pp. 201–202.

14. Kagan, p. 25.

CHAPTER 3. VYING FOR POLITICAL POWER

1. Plutarch, *Pericles*, in *Rise and Fall of Athens: Nine Greek Lives by Plutarch*, trans. Ian Scott-Kilvert (New York: Penguin, 1960), p. 171.

2. Kagan, *Pericles of Athens and the Birth of Democracy* (New York: Free Press, 1991), p. 27.

3. Plutarch, *Life of Cimon*, in *Rise and Fall of Athens: Nine Greek Lives by Plutarch*, pp. 145–146.

4. Aristotle, *The Athenian Constitution*, trans. H. Rackham (Cambridge, Mass.: Harvard University Press, 1952, reprint 1996), p. 129.

5. Plutarch, *Life of Cimon*, p. 151.

6. Aeschylus, "The Persians," in *Prometheus Bound, The Suppliants, Seven Against Thebes, The Persians*, trans. Philip Vellacott (Baltimore: Penguin, 1961), p. 134.

CHAPTER 4. ENORMOUS AMBITIONS IN ATHENS

1. Plutarch, *Pericles*, in *Rise and Fall of Athens: Nine Greek Lives by Plutarch*, trans. Ian Scott-Kilvert (New York: Penguin, 1960), p. 183.

2. Ibid., p. 183.

3. Ibid., p. 182.

4. Ibid., p. 183.

5. Ibid., pp. 171–172.

6. Ibid., pp. 172–173.

7. Donald Kagan, *The Outbreak of the Peloponnesian War* (Ithaca, New York: Cornell University Press 1969), p. 127.

8. Thucydides, *Peloponnesian War*, trans. Rex Warner (New York: Penguin, 1972) p. 93.

9. Ibid., p. 96.

10. Plutarch, *Pericles*, p. 173.

11. Thucydides, p. 97.

12. Plutarch, *Pericles*, p. 175.

13. Ibid., p. 175.

14. Plutarch, *Pericles*, p. 161.

CHAPTER 5. PROMOTING DEMOCRACY AND CULTURE

1. Thucydides, *Peloponnesian War*, trans. Rex Warner (New York: Penguin, 1972), p. 148.

2. Kagan, *Pericles of Athens*, p. 47.

3. Thucydides, p. 147.

4. Old Oligarch, *Constitution of the Athenians*, in Xenophon, Scripta Minora, trans. E. C. Marchant (Cambridge, Mass.: Harvard University Press, 1993), p. 479.

5. Old Oligarch, p. 477.

6. Thucydides, pp. 147–149.

7. Plutarch, *Pericles*, in *Rise and Fall of Athens: Nine Greek Lives by Plutarch*, trans. Ian Scott-Kilvert (New York: Penguin, 1960), p. 178.

8. Plutarch, *Pericles*, p. 178.

9. Ibid., p. 178.

10. Ibid., p. 177.

11. Ibid., pp. 178–179.

12. Pausanias, *Guide to Greece, 2 Volumes*, trans. Peter Levi (New York: Penguin, 1971), vol. 1, p. 75.

13. Pausanias, "Guide to Greece," excerpted in J. J. Pollitt, ed. and trans., *The Art of Ancient Greece: Sources and Documents* (New York: Cambridge University Press, 1990), p. 56.

14. John Miliadis, *The Acropolis* (Athens: M. Pechlivanidis, n.d.), p. 14.

CHAPTER 6. TROUBLES WITH FAMILY AND FRIENDS

1. Plutarch, *Pericles*, in *Rise and Fall of Athens: Nine Greek Lives by Plutarch*, trans. Ian Scott-Kilvert (New York: Penguin, 1960), p. 181.

2. Xenophon, "Oeconomicus," in *Xenophon: Conversations With Socrates*, trans. Hugh Tredennick and Robin Waterfield (New York: Penguin, 1990), pp. 311–312.

3. Plato, "Protagoras," in *Plato*, trans. Benjamin Jowett (Chicago: Encyclopedia Britannica, 1952), p. 47.

4. Plutarch, *Pericles*, p. 202.

5. Plutarch, *Life of Alcibiades*, in *Rise and Fall of Athens,* pp. 245–246.

6. Ibid., p. 246.

7. Ibid., p. 250.

8. Xenophon, "Memorabilia," in *Xenophon: Conversations With Socrates*, trans. Hugh Tredennick and Robin Waterfield (New York: Penguin, 1990), pp. 80–81.

9. Plutarch, *Pericles*, pp. 190–191.

10. Robert B. Kebric, *Greek People* (Mountain View, Calif.: Mayfield, 2005), p. 175.

11. Plutarch, *Pericles*, p. 198.

12. Ibid., p. 198.

13. Kagan, pp. 185–186.

14. Plutarch, *Pericles*, p. 198.

CHAPTER 7. ON THE ROAD TO TOTAL WAR

1. Plutarch, *Pericles*, in *Rise and Fall of Athens: Nine Greek Lives by Plutarch*, trans. Ian Scott-Kilvert (New York: Penguin, 1960), p. 194.

2. Thucydides, *Peloponnesian War,* trans. Rex Warner (New York: Penguin, 1972), pp. 50–51.

3. Ibid., p. 54.

4. Ibid., p. 56.

5. Ibid., pp. 61–62.

6. Plutarch, *Pericles*, p. 195.

7. Kagan, *Pericles of Athens and the Birth of Democracy* (New York: Free Press, 1991), p. 201.

8. Thucydides, pp. 66–67.

9. Ibid., pp. 67.

10. Ibid., p. 63–64.

11. Ibid., pp. 73–74.

12. Ibid., p. 76.

13. Ibid., pp. 76–77.

14. Ibid., pp. 82–84.

15. Plutarch, p. 196.

16. Thucydides, pp. 86–87.

CHAPTER 8. WAR POLICY AND DEMISE

1. Thucydides, *Peloponnesian War*, trans. Rex Warner (New York: Penguin, 1972), p. 118.

2. Ibid., pp. 119, 123.

3. Ibid., p. 35.

4. Ibid., p. 138.

5. Plutarch, *Pericles*, in *Rise and Fall of Athens: Nine Greek Lives by Plutarch*, trans. Ian Scott-Kilvert (New York: Penguin, 1960), p. 200.

6. Donald Kagan, *The Peloponnesian War* (New York: Viking, 2003), p. 69.

7. Thucydides, p. 142.

8. Ibid., p. 143.

9. Ibid., pp. 145, 147–148.

10. Ibid., p. 146.

11. Ibid., pp. 149–150.

12. Ibid., pp. 152–153.

13. Plutarch, *Pericles*, p. 201.

14. Thucydides, pp. 154–155.

15. Ibid., p. 203.

16. Ibid., p. 204.

17. Ibid., pp. 204–205.

18. Ibid., pp. 205–206.

CHAPTER 9. PERICLES' LEGACY

1. Thucydides, *Peloponnesian War*, trans. Rex Warner (New York: Penguin, 1972), p. 163.

2. Plutarch, *Life of Nicias*, in *Rise and Fall of Athens: Nine Greek Lives by Plutarch*, trans. Ian Scott-Kilvert (New York: Penguin, 1960), p. 109.

3. Kagan, *Pericles of Athens and the Birth of Democracy* (New York: Free Press, 1991), p. 3.

4. Plutarch, "Pericles," p. 179.

5. Ibid., p. 167.

6. Miliadis, *Acropolis* (Athens: M. Pechlivanidis, n.d.), p. 6.

GLOSSARY

ACROPOLIS—"The city's high place"; a hill, usually fortified, central to many Greek towns; the term in uppercase (Acropolis) refers to the one in Athens.

ARCHON—In many Greek states, including Athens, a public administrator.

AREOPAGUS—A hill in Athens on which an aristocratic council of the same name met.

ASSEMBLY—In many ancient Greek states, a meeting of citizens for the purpose of electing leaders, discussing issues, and/or passing laws; the term in uppercase (Assembly) refers to the one in Athens.

ATHENA PARTHENOS—"Athena the virgin;" the giant statue of Athena that stood inside the Parthenon temple.

BOULE—The council made up of five hundred citizens and charged with creating legislative bills and carrying out the directives of the Assembly.

CELLA—The main room of a Greek temple, usually housing the cult image (statue) of the god to whom the temple was dedicated.

CHOREGUS (PLURAL CHOREGOI)—A wealthy backer of plays and other theatrical and cultural events.

DEMOCRACY—A political system in which the people or their representatives make the laws and govern the state.

DEMOS—In ancient Athens, a collective word for all of the city's citizens.

HELOT—An agricultural serf in ancient Sparta. The helots endured poor living conditions and sometimes physical abuse.

HOPLITES—In ancient Greece, heavily armored infantry soldiers who fought with thrusting spears and short swords.

IONIA—The region encompassing the coasts of western Asia Minor (now Turkey) and nearby islands, where many Greek cities flourished.

LITURGIES—In ancient Athens and some other Greek city-states, public duties assumed by wealthy citizens, such as paying for feasts at religious festivals.

METIC—In ancient Athens, a resident foreigner, either a Greek from another city-state or a non-Greek. Metics had fewer civic rights than Athenian citizens.

OSTRACISM—A democratic procedure developed in Athens in which the citizens voted to banish an unpopular leader.

PAIDAGOGOS—A slave or servant who accompanied a Greek boy to school and oversaw his behavior.

PENTEKONTEITIA—The "Fifty Years;" the period encompassing the mid-part of the fifth century B.C. in which Athens reached its political and cultural height.

PHALANX—A formidable military formation in which infantrymen bearing spears and shields stood in ranks (lines), one behind the other.

POLEMARCH—Originally the commander-in-chief of the Athenian army, but by the fifth century B.C. a civilian official in charge of lawsuits involving foreigners.

PROBOULEUMETA—In ancient Athens, legislative bills drawn up by the Council and voted on by the Assembly.

STRATEGOS (PLURAL IS STRATEGOI)—One of ten generals elected yearly in ancient Athens.

TRIREME—A warship having three banks of oars.

FURTHER READING

Aird, Hamish. *Pericles: The Rise and Fall of Athenian Democracy*. New York: Rosen, 2004.

Apel, Melanie Ann. *Art and Religion in Ancient Greece*. New York: PowerKids Press, 2004.

Barter, James. *The Ancient Persians*. San Diego, Calif.: Lucent Books, 2005.

Connolly, Peter. *Ancient Greece*. New York: Oxford University Press, 2001.

Curlee, Lynn. *Parthenon*. New York: Atheneum Books for Young Readers, 2004.

Kebric, Robert B. *Greek People*. Mountain View, Calif.: Mayfield, 2005.

Kerrigan, Michael. *Ancient Greece and the Mediterranean*. New York: Dorling Kindersley, 2001.

Nardo, Don, *Greek Temples*. New York: Franklin Watts, 2002.

———. *Life in Ancient Athens*. San Diego: Lucent Books, 2000.

————. *Women of Ancient Greece*. San Diego: Lucent Books, 2000.

Roberts, Jennifer and Tracy Barrett. *The Ancient Greek World*. New York: Oxford University Press, 2004.

Shuter, Jane. *Life in a Greek Temple*. Chicago, Ill.: Heinemann Library, 2005.

Whiting, Jim. *The Life and Times of Pericles*. Hockessin, Del.: Mitchell Land Publishers, 2005.

INTERNET ADDRESSES

CLASSICAL GREEK ARCHITECTURE

An excellent photo site that focuses on the great buildings of the Classical Age, including the Parthenon and other structures sponsored by Pericles.

<http://harpy.uccs.edu>

Under "Image Collections," click on "Greek." Select "Architecture."

THE GREEKS: THE DEMOCRATIC EXPERIMENT

The BBC provides this excellent site describing ancient Greek democracy, with a text by the noted scholar Paul Cartledge.

<http://www.bbc.co.uk>

Scroll down and click on "History" under "Other BBC sites." Under "Topics," select "Ancient History." Click on "Greeks." Scroll down and select "The Democractic Experiment."

PERSEUS PROJECT

The most comprehensive online source about ancient Greece, with hundreds of links to all aspects of Greek history, life, and culture, supported by numerous photos of artifacts.

<http://www.perseus.tufts.edu>

INDEX